SLEEPING WITH THE LIGHTS ON

the unsettling story of horror

DARRYL JONES

Sleeping with the Lights On

SLEEPING WITH
THE LIGHTS ON

the unsettling story of horror

DARRYL JONES

OXFORD
UNIVERSITY PRESS

OXFORD

UNIVERSITY PRESS

Great Clarendon Street, Oxford, OX2 6DP,
United Kingdom

Oxford University Press is a department of the University of Oxford.
It furthers the University's objective of excellence in research, scholarship,
and education by publishing worldwide. Oxford is a registered trade mark of
Oxford University Press in the UK and in certain other countries

First Edition published in 2018

Impression: 1

Cover and chapter opener images: Shutterstock.com

Published in the United States of America by Oxford University Press
198 Madison Avenue, New York, NY 10016, United States of America

British Library Cataloguing in Publication Data

Data available

Library of Congress Control Number: 2018937070

ISBN 978-0-19-882648-4

Printed and bound in China by
C&C Offset Printing Co., Ltd.

To Margaret and Morgan
with all my love in a world of horror

CONTENTS

ACKNOWLEDGEMENTS

I have been thinking about a book like this for years. I would like to thank Jenny Nugee at OUP for giving me the opportunity to turn this from an imaginary book to an actual one, and for her patience while I tried to do it. The anonymous reviewers at OUP made many helpful suggestions, and helped to give shape and form to this book.

I have the best colleagues, who are the best friends. I am enormously grateful to Bernice Murphy, who read and commented on the manuscript with such generosity of time and spirit. This book is very much the better for her advice. I have had so many conversations about so many things for so many years with Jarlath Killeen, and the record of some of them can be found in these pages. Eve Patten has been a constant source of moral and intellectual support.

I would also like to thank Mary Bridgeman, Ailise Bulfin, John Connolly, Nick Curwin, Nick Daly, Ruth Doherty, Dara Downey, Triona Kirby, Miles Link, Judith Luna, Elizabeth McCarthy, Orla McCarthy, Ben Murnane, Sorcha Ní Fhlainn, Ed O'Hare, Maria Parsons, and Conor Reid, all of whom have made contributions to this book in their different ways. Valerie Smith, Cathy Gibson, Shumane Cleary, Marian

Acknowledgements

Harte, Eimear Leonard, Laura Cusack, and Jade Barreto have kept me sane and kept me going for the past few years.

As ever, the first, last, and deepest debts of love and gratitude are to my wife, Margaret Robson, and my daughter, Morgan Jones. This horrid book is for them.

LIST OF FIGURES

Introduction

Horror in Civilization

A human eyeball shoots out of its socket, and rolls into a gutter. A child returns from the dead and tears the beating heart from his tormentor's chest. A young man has horrifying visions of his decomposing mother's corpse. A baby is ripped from its living mother's womb. A mother tears her son to pieces, and parades around with his head on a stick. These are scenes from the notorious, banned 'video nasty' films (a series of controversial, violent VHS releases prohibited in the UK under the Video Recordings Act of 1984) *Eaten Alive*, *Zombie Flesh Eaters*, *I Spit on Your Grave*, *Anthropophagous: The Beast*, and *Cannibal Holocaust*.

Well, no. They could be—but they're not. All these scenes and images can be found in any bookshop, safely inside the respectable covers of canonical literary classics, in the works of Edgar Allan Poe, M. R. James, James Joyce, William Shakespeare, and Euripides. Only the first two of these are avowedly writers of horror, and none of these books comes with any kind of public health warning or age-suitability guideline. What is the relationship between culture and violence?

1

Figure 1. Death of Pentheus, from *The Bacchae*, Greek Vase *c*.480 BC.

Euripides' *The Bacchae*, first performed around 400 BC, is one of the foundational works of the Western literary canon. In describing graphically the actions of Agave and her Maenads, dismembering King Pentheus while under the frenzied influence of the god Dionysus, and putting his head on a pole, it also sets the bar very high for artistic representations of violence and gore (Figure 1). The spectacle of violence, then, is encoded in art from its very beginnings. Palaeohistorians have argued plausibly that the capacity to make art is one of the crucial distinguishing features of humanity, and a very significant evolutionary advantage: *Homo sapiens* made art, we survived; Neanderthals did neither. It is likely that Greek tragedy and perhaps all art has its deep origins in ritual. The anthropologist Clifford Geertz usefully defines ritual as 'consecrated behavior', and suggests that elaborate or public religious rituals might best be thought of as 'cultural performances', simultaneously providing both models *of* an external or social reality (they *reflect* reality) and models *for* that reality (they *shape* reality). We will return to the ritualistic element of horror throughout this book, but for now I want to give an example of the interweaving of culture, religion, and horror.

Pier Paolo Pasolini's *Medea* (1969) is a free adaptation of Euripides' tragedy of the same name, directed by a major European film-maker and intellectual, and starring the legendary operatic diva Maria Callas in the title role. It is, in other words, unmistakeably a high-cultural artistic product, deeply influenced by Pasolini's own studies in anthropology, mythography, and religious history, and by his Marxist politics. But this is art-house cinema red in tooth and claw. Shot in the beautiful unearthly volcanic landscape around Göreme in Cappadocia, Turkey, the film opens with a *sparagmos*, a graphically rendered ritual sacrifice: a young boy is killed and dismembered, his blood and body parts cast over the land in order to assure its fertility. In travelling to the ends of the earth—to Colchis, in what is today Georgia—to retrieve the Golden Fleece, the film suggests, Jason is also symbolically travelling back in time, to witness the origins of civilization in a religion of magic, ritual, and human sacrifice. Jason takes Medea back with him to Corinth, the city state of modernity and intrigue (these scenes are filmed in Pisa), but Medea carries the primal world within her (she lives beyond the *polis*, outside the city walls), and this enables her to summon up the appalling forces of vengeance, the Furies, in order to kill her own children.

The film's opening episode of human sacrifice is unquestionably a shocking scene in itself, but for certain viewers
of horror cinema it is also a disorientating one, as it clearly
prefigures, both aesthetically and thematically, some of
the most controversial films ever made. *Medea*'s *sparagmos*
closely resembles (or anticipates) a number of scenes of
ritual human sacrifice and dismemberment from Ruggero
Deodato's *Cannibal Holocaust* (1980), Umberto Lenzi's *Cannibal Ferox* (1981), and a number of other Italian cannibal
movies of the late 1970s and early 1980s. Unlike *Medea*, all of
these films were banned under the Video Recordings Act of
1984. *Cannibal Holocaust*, in particular, has an infamous place
in popular demonology as perhaps the archetypal 'video
nasty'. It is a film so powerful, and for many so unacceptable,
that its director was arrested and tried shortly after its
release, on charges not only of obscenity but also of murder,
as the authorities initially refused to believe that the film's
scenes of violence and torture could possibly have been
staged. (They were, and Deodato was acquitted when the
actors involved were revealed to be alive and well.)

The episode of the baby ripped from the mother's womb
to which I alluded in the first paragraph is from *Macbeth*,
of course—it's Macduff's account of his own birth. And
Macbeth, though certainly no slouch in the mayhem department, isn't even Shakespeare's most violent play. That
would be *Titus Andronicus*, whose opening scene makes the
connections between civilization and horror very clear: the
origins of civilization are in violence; ritual and other
forms of sacred violence are used to channel otherwise
uncontrollably violent, destabilizing urges into socially

licensed forms. At the beginning of *Titus Andronicus*, Tamora, Queen of the Goths, sees her son brutally killed by the conquering Romans:

> See, lord and father, how we have performed
> Our Roman rites: Alarbus' limbs are lopp'd,
> And entrails feed the sacrificing fire,
> Whose smoke, like incense, doth perfume the sky.

What follows is well known: further mutilation, rape, cannibalism—the full Jacobean panoply. Shocking, yes; surprising, no. After all, the greater part of the Western literary tradition follows, or celebrates, a faith whose own sacrificial rites have at their heart symbolic representations of torture and cannibalism, the cross and the host. A case could plausibly be made that the Western literary tradition *is* a tradition of horror. This may be an overstatement, but it's an argument with which any honest thinker has to engage.

The classic argument in defence of the brutality of tragedy (a form which I have come to think of as highbrow horror) is the Aristotelian concept of *catharsis*, according to which the act of witnessing artistic representations of cruelty and monstrosity, pity and fear, purges the audience of these emotions, leaving them psychologically healthier. *Horror is good for you!* I confess I have always had difficulty accepting this hypothesis (though I recognize that many people far more learned and brilliant than me have had no trouble accepting it). It seems to me to be a classic example of an intellectual's gambit, a theory offered without recourse to any evidence.

And yet catharsis seems to me to be far preferable to another, more common, response to horror: the urge to censor or ban extreme documents and images in the name of public morality. If catharsis is Aristotelian, then this hypothesis is Pavlovian: horror conditions our responses; a tendency to watch violent acts leads inexorably to a tendency to commit violent acts. For many people, this seems to make intuitive sense (on more than one occasion, I've noticed people backing away from me when I tell them I work on horror), and it's the impetus behind the framing of the Video Recordings Act of 1984, after which *Cannibal Holocaust* and all those other video nasties were banned.

As a number of commentators and critics have noted, there's no evidence for this Pavlovian hypothesis, either. Worse than that, there's a distinct class animus behind such thinking. You and I, cultured, literate, educated middle-class folks that we are, are perfectly safe: when we watch *Cannibal Holocaust* (which I do, even if you don't) we know what we are seeing, we can contextualize the film, interpret it, recognize it for what it is. The problem, the argument implicitly goes, is not us, it is *them*, those festering, semi-bestial proletarians whose extant propensity for violence (always simmering beneath the surface) can only be stoked by watching these films. That's why no one seriously considers banning *The Bacchae* or *Titus Andronicus*—why any suggestion that we do so would be treated as an act of inexcusable philistinism. They are horror for the educated classes.

Horror is, unquestionably, an extreme art form. Like all avant-garde art, I would suggest, its real purpose is to force its audiences to confront the limits of their own tolerance—including, emphatically, their own tolerance for what is or is not art. Commonly, when hitting these limits, we respond with fear, frustration, and even rage. Even today, this is not an unusual reaction on first reading *Finnegans Wake*, for example: I see it occasionally in my students, who are (a) voluntarily students of literature; and (b) usually Irish, not to say actual Dubliners. So we shouldn't be surprised that audiences respond to horror with—well, horror. But we need to recognize that the reasons for doing this are complex, and are deeply bound up with the meaning and function of art, and of civilization. Horror runs very deep, and is part of what we are.

'Gothic', 'Horror', and 'Terror'

These are terms which recur in thinking and writing about our subject, sometimes used interchangeably, and certainly often defined and understood very loosely. In many ways this is understandable, as a too-rigid taxonomy can lead to an inability to see the wood for the trees. I will be using the umbrella term 'horror' throughout this book to signify a variety of artistic genres and cultural forms, modes, and moods, some of which are, if not incompatible with one another, then certainly contradictory in their aims and effects. Nevertheless, it is important to establish a reasonably clear sense of what commentators mean when they use the terms 'Gothic', 'horror', and 'terror'.

The Gothic is a cultural and aesthetic mode associated with and expressive of darkness and death, irrationality and obsession, sensuality and disorder, the past and its mysteries.

The Gothic is always dressed in black. Fred Botting's famous assertion that 'Gothic signifies a writing of excess' is perceptive but incomplete. There is certainly something excessive about the Gothic—a *transgression* of aesthetic propriety or social respectability, an *overpouring* of emotion, an *obsession* with madness, the unconscious, and extreme psychological states. All of these statements suggest that the Gothic bursts through or exists beyond the boundaries of respectable society—of bourgeois capitalism and the literary and artistic form which grew to give it expression, realism.

But one of the Gothic's many excesses is an excess of *definition*. It has become an overdetermined signifier, a word with too much meaning. As Nick Groom notes in *The Gothic: A Very Short Introduction*, the term 'Gothic' can be used to refer to ethnography, architecture, literature, youth subculture, fashion, music, and much else besides. It is a major cultural mode, and an *oppositional* one. The original Goths were a Germanic people who harried the Roman Empire and made serious incursions into its territories in the first millennium AD. Gothic in this sense is to be understood as a force acting in opposition to the civilizing *polis* and order of Rome, signifying wildness, disorder, 'barbarism'. Medieval Gothic architecture, a primarily ecclesiastical form characterized by a soaring use of light and space and an ostentatious asymmetry of design and ornament, is understood as existing in opposition to the balance, symmetry, and simplicity of classical architectural forms. Similarly, the outrageously ornate styles of Victorian neo-Gothic architecture were themselves developed in opposition to the rational symmetry, balance, and harmony of Enlightenment neoclassical architecture. As part of the same reaction, in the latter part of the eighteenth century, the Gothic novel, with its recurring focus on darkness and decay, madness and the past, developed alongside and in opposition to the classic realist novel. In their dress and music, modern Goths clearly define themselves in opposition to middle-class social respectability.

The continuing popularity and success of the Gothic is in part an acknowledgement that there are whole areas of human existence about which realism has little or nothing to say: extreme psychological states and the limits of consciousness, for example; or profound existential, metaphysical, or spiritual questions; the paranormal and the supernatural. In its scrutiny of the limits of rationalism, horror in general has often drawn upon the concept of the sublime, first theorized in classical antiquity by 'Longinus' (we don't know the exact name of the author), but given a powerful new articulation in the eighteenth century. In 1757, the Irish politician and philosopher Edmund Burke published what was to become one of the key intellectual documents of Romanticism, and one of the most important works of aesthetics of its time, *A Philosophical Enquiry Into the Origin of Our Ideas of the Sublime and Beautiful*. The sublime, Burke argued, was a fundamentally metaphysical, or even numinous, category (that is, one infused with the divine), short-circuiting reason completely in its presentation of images and spectacles so vast, so overwhelming, that they produced an effect of reverent awe, and even terror, in those who experienced them. Pain, Burke wrote, is 'an emissary of the king of terrors'—Death—and thus:

> Whatever is fitted in any sort to excite the ideas of pain, and danger, that is to say, whatever is in any sort terrible, or is conversant about terrible objects, or operates in a manner analogous to terror, is a source of the *sublime*; that is, it is productive of the strongest emotion which the mind is capable of feeling.

The Burkean sublime was to become a central concept for understanding the Gothic. In 1826 Ann Radcliffe, the most celebrated Gothic novelist of her generation, and one of the pioneering figures in modern horror, outlined what was to become an important distinction for many theorists of the form, between 'terror' (metaphysical dread) and 'horror' (shocking, often disgusting revelation):

> Terror and horror are so far opposite, that the first expands the soul, and awakens the faculties to a high degree of life; the other contracts, freezes, and nearly annihilates them. I apprehend, that neither Shakspeare [*sic*] nor Milton by their fictions, nor Mr. Burke by his reasoning, anywhere looked to positive horror as a source of the sublime, though they all agree that terror is a very high one; and where lies the great difference between horror and terror, but in the uncertainty and obscurity, that accompany the first, respecting the dreaded evil?

Though not all commentators accept it, the distinction between terror and horror has proved lasting and influential. For example, Stephen King, by far the most prominent living horror writer, makes it one of the cornerstones of his analysis of the genre in his important study, *Danse Macabre* (1981): 'So: terror on top, horror below it, and lowest of all, the gag reflex of revulsion.... I recognize terror as the finest emotion...and so I will try to terrorize the reader. But if I find I cannot terrify him/her, I will try to horrify; and if I find I cannot horrify, I'll go for the gross-out. I'm not proud.'

To offer some generalization, to which there are always counterexamples: 'terror' poses existential questions for the audience as to the nature of reality, the validity of their beliefs, the reliability of perception. It is often expressed in the paranormal or supernatural, in 'things which should not be', in challenges to the integrity of the self (the doppelgänger) or the arrow of time (precognition, 'we have been here before'). It is productive of fear. 'Horror' might best be thought of as embodied, corporeal, articulated through pain or through the dissolution of the flesh. It can be productive of shock.

King's identification of 'the gross-out' as the lowest form of horror is an interesting one. The desire to make your audience puke may not be a very exalted artistic aim, but it is an artistic aim nevertheless. The aesthetics of disgust are real, and governed by powerful taboos. My mouth is full of saliva, which I swallow all the time, and yet I would not readily drink a glass of milk into which I have just spat. The social and intellectual origins of these taboos have been the subject of an influential analysis by the anthropologist Mary Douglas in her book *Purity and Danger* (1966). Douglas writes:

> The body is a model which can stand for any bounded system. Its boundaries can represent any boundaries which are

11

> threatened or precarious. The body is a complex structure. The functions of its different parts and their relation afford a source of symbols for other complex structures. We cannot possibly interpret rituals concerning excreta, breast milk, saliva and the rest unless we are prepared to see in the body a symbol of society, and to see the powers and dangers credited to the social structure reproduced in small on the human body.

For Douglas, social and mental organization seeks *order*, a clear classification and categorization of events and objects. Pollution and taboo occur at the margins of these categories, or in the interstices (spaces) between them, the cognitive and categorical gaps: 'bodily margins [are] thought to be specially invested with power and danger . . . [because] all margins are dangerous. If they are pulled this way or that the shape of fundamental experience is altered. Any structure of ideas is vulnerable at its margins.' Horror, then, occurs at the boundaries of these clear category distinctions, where our sense of certainty, integrity, unity is suddenly profoundly challenged, destabilized. Self/other, living/dead, male/ female, adult/child, human/non-human, inside/outside, solid/liquid—as we will see many times in this book, horror tests the limits or margins of these (and other) categories, and in doing so tests our responses to them. Our skin, for example, is a clear boundary between self/other, inside/out- side, living/dead. These binaries are clearly transgressed when the skin is ruptured or breached (slashed) by external trauma: what is outside should stay outside. But the con- verse is in its way equally traumatic. What is inside can become taboo, polluted, abject when it crosses the boundary of the flesh, as in the case of my saliva in the glass of milk.

Urine, blood, mucus, shit, pus are all abject once outside. This explains horror's recurring fascination with a variety of abject substances, often viscous materials which violate clear solid/liquid boundaries—blood, gore, goo, slime, drool, guts, vomit, semen, menses. In horror, all of these are, in their various ways, matter in the wrong place. This also explains horror's recurring imagistic and symbolic fascination with the body's orifices, its permeable boundaries between self and other, inside and outside, its points of anxiety and doubt: the mouth, the vagina, the anus, the eyes. From the *vagina dentata*—the vagina with teeth—to the related image of the vampire's fanged, red mouth, to the eyeball piercings of *King Lear*, Luis Bunuel's *Un Chien Andalou*, or *Zombie Flesh Eaters*, horror is full of such images.

Perhaps understandably, then, horror's violation of taboos can often be seen as an affront to decency. While the products of horror can often be readily incorporated into capitalism, always eager to commodify its own dissent (*Twilight* is an obvious modern example), nevertheless part of the power of horror lies in its transgressive nature. It can be, as I suggested, an avant-garde art form, whose function is to shock us out of our respectability and complacency—*épater la bourgeoisie* (to shock the middle classes), as French *fin-de-siècle* poets put it. Since it probes at the boundaries of the ethics of representation (what can or cannot be shown, what should or should not be articulated), the history of horror is also the history of outraged responses to horror, of censorship, moral panics, video nasty scandals, and other forms of social and political anxiety. Some practitioners of horror have, in turn, drawn strength and inspiration from the edginess of their relationship with censorship, as in the case of Clive Barker: 'Paradoxically, I thank God for them [censors]. I think it's important that there should always be somebody around who says that this is forbidden territory. We are, after all, trading on taboo.' When horror gets too respectable, too near the mainstream, it can lose much of its power.

Horror brings us face to face with our own flesh, our corporeality, and with the mutability and malleability of that flesh, its softness, its porousness or leakiness, its vulnerability, its appalling potential for pain, its capacity for metamorphosis or decay, its stinkiness and putridity, its transience and mortality. Etymologically, horror originally signified an involuntary embodied response: it derives from the Latin *horrere*, 'to stand on end', 'to bristle' (hence *horripilation*: hair standing on end; goose flesh). From its original definition of hair standing on end, *horrere* came to mean *to shake, to tremble, to shudder at, to dread, to be afraid of*, and conversely *to be frightful, be terrible, be desolate*.

On Halloween 1990, the BBC broadcast *Horror Café*, a panel discussion which brought together different practitioners of horror, writers and film-makers, from different traditions and generations. Among them was the horror *auteur* John Carpenter, director of *Halloween*, *The Fog*, *The Thing*, and many others, who made the following observation:

> There's an essential question that you have to answer, and it's basic when you make a film. There's two kinds of [horror]. There's a left-wing horror and a right-wing horror. Now, the right-wing horror—we're all a tribe, and the evil is out *there*. [Points to the distance.] It's gonna come and get

us.... There's also a left-wing horror, and it's right in *here*.
[Points to his chest.]

Carpenter's comment here astutely brings together two ostensibly different issues: the *politics* of horror and the *location* of horror. Horror can be, I have argued, an intensely political form, but its politics are not uniform. Some horror is, we have seen, radical and avant-garde, deliberately oppositional, setting out as a matter of central policy to shock, to affront sensibilities, to undermine authority.

This idea of radical horror is not misguided or wrong, but it *is* partial. Stephen King, incomparably the most influential and successful living horror writer, recognized that for him horror spoke to the 'inner Republican'. It's a subversive conservatism, perhaps, with undeniable streaks of rebellion, but nevertheless a conservatism marshalled in the service of an agenda that can only be called traditionalist. 'In my character', King writes in his extraordinarily revealing 'Memoir of the Craft', *On Writing*, 'a kind of wildness and a deep conservatism are wound together like hair in a braid'. Horror, we will see, can emerge from intensely conservative values, ranging from the comfort and convention of traditional ghost stories, to a genre such as the slasher movie, which in its original form tended to police the sexual behaviour of its teenage cast with extraordinary severity, presenting a world in which the punishment for premarital sex was a violent death. For some kinds of horror, threats to order are everywhere; they need to be contained, controlled, or preferably destroyed. Horror as a cultural form maintains a dialogic relationship between radicalism (the urge to confront) and conservatism (the desire to control).

Horror occupies extreme terrain—it deals in shock and outrage, nausea and abjection, fear and loathing. And yet it is also a highly pleasurable genre. The large popular audiences for horror movies don't just go along to have their souls harrowed or their lunch returned. They certainly don't go, as some censorious accounts of horror would suggest, because they are sick people in search of ideas and in need of psychological treatment. They go because they *enjoy* horror. Horripilation can be a pleasurable experience. In Jane Austen's quasi-Gothic *Northanger Abbey*, Henry Tilney reads Ann Radcliffe: 'The Mysteries of Udolpho, when I had once begun it, I could not lay down again;—I remember finishing it in two days—my hair standing on end the whole time.' Horror audiences laugh as often as they scream, or laugh and scream at the same time.

The pleasures of genre are, in fact, often akin to those of ritual. They are based on repetition, on the acting out of predetermined roles, on the precise fulfilment of expectations. Horror audiences are often highly knowledgeable, with an acute intuitive knowledge of the codes and conventions of the genre. They often know *exactly* what to expect, and this explains the enduring popularity of many of the most generically formulaic kinds of horror, from Radcliffe's Gothic novels to slasher movies. Nobody went to see *Friday the 13th, part 8*, or *Saw 6*, expecting a whole new cinematic experience from the one they got when they went to see *Friday the 13th, part 7*, or *Saw 5*. Sometimes, this genre-familiarity can indeed lend a ritualistic or even a participatory experience to the work or art, as we go self-consciously through the conventions of the genre while experiencing it, or even start to take part in the work ourselves (like the audience for *The Rocky Horror Picture Show*). The great success of the *Scream* franchise (1996–2011), for example, is to a large extent predicated on its audience's genre expertise. We have been here before.

The Uncanny and the Weird

We have all experienced moments, or feelings, in which the world is suddenly not quite as we thought it was—in which that which was familiar is suddenly revealed to us as strange, or that which was strange suddenly seems familiar. These experiences can be disconcerting, leading to a sense of unease, in which our certainties momentarily dissolve, to give a sense of a quite different reality or order of existence. In this mood of uncertainty, we can no longer be sure of our own senses, of our secure interpretation of reality based on an accumulated lifetime of experiences. We begin to question the nature of that reality: Did I just see that, or didn't I? What's that noise? Is someone outside? Wasn't that door closed the last time I looked? Am I alone in the house? Why do I keep getting the sense of a presence, just over my shoulder? Is someone—or something—following me? Am I going mad?

This feeling of existential uncertainty is called the *uncanny*, and is a familiar one to readers and viewers of horror. It is a category which was famously discussed by Sigmund Freud in his 1919 essay, 'The "Uncanny"'. 'Uncanny' here is a translation of the German word *unheimlich*, which literally means something like 'unhomely'. This suggests a common definition of the uncanny as that which is strange, unfamiliar, 'far from home'. And yet Freud suggests that the uncanny occurs when the meaning of *unheimlich* collapses into its opposite, *heimlich* (homely)—when the strange and the familiar meet.

This, for example, can refer to family secrets, things which are kept locked up at home, from madwomen in the attic to prisoners in the cellar. Some of the horror we will encounter in this book arises out of a worry that apparently bland facades—the handsome face, the suburban front door, the kindly landlady—might conceal monstrous interiors. The haunted house is in some ways a literalizing of the uncanny—a place of security and welcome becomes a place of terror and desolation. Some of the most successful ghost stories turn on this undecideability. An enormous reservoir of critical ink, for example, has been expended in analysing whether Henry James's *The Turn of the Screw* is a supernatural tale of a haunted house, or a psychological tale whose narrator imagines ghosts as an aspect of her mental breakdown. (The answer, it seems to me, is that the story derives its uncanny power from the simultaneous existence of *both* interpretations.)

Some other uncanny tales play on a creeping awareness that reality is unstable. As we have seen, horror often arises out of a blurring or transgressing of clear category distinctions. The uncanny tends to arise out of a sense of uncertainty as to whether we are encountering or experiencing something which is alive or dead, organic or inert, material or supernatural. It is the statue that moves, the portrait whose eyes follow you around the room, the doll that comes to life, the mirror that reflects back a different room, or a different face, the door that suddenly will not open, or that opens of its own accord, or that rattles as if being violently shaken from the outside when you know there's no one there. It is the window that looks out onto an unexpectedly strange vista, or onto nothing at all.

If the uncanny is a sudden glimpse into the possibility of the supernatural, then what is often called the *weird* arises out of a sense that the material world is degrees of magnitude larger and more complex than we could possibly have imagined, and that it contains and far exceeds any conception we might have of the supernatural. The weird often stresses the *insignificance* of humanity, as in this celebrated observation in the opening paragraph of H. P. Lovecraft's 'The Call of Cthulhu':

> The most merciful thing in the world, I think, is the inability of the human mind to correlate all its contents. We live on a placid island of ignorance in the midst of black seas of infinity, and it was not meant that we should voyage far. The sciences, each straining in its own direction, have hitherto harmed us little, but some day the piecing together of dissociated knowledge will open up such terrifying vistas of reality, and of our frightful position therein, that we shall either go mad from the revelation or flee from the deadly light into the peace and safety of a new dark age.

The theorist Mark Fisher suggests that the weird arises from 'a fascination for the outside, for that which lies beyond standard perception, cognition and experience'. The human brain simply cannot comprehend all of the Real, and thus we have developed an extremely limited and finite comforting 'reality', rather like our ability only to see visible light, a tiny slice of the vast spectrum of waves, or the fact that our senses confine us to three dimensions when mathematicians and physicists tell us that there are many more. Following Lovecraft, and particularly his creation of the kraken-god Cthulhu, weird fiction has developed an obsession with transdimensional invertebrate life forms, with a particular emphasis on the utterly inhuman morphology of cephalopods. Weird fiction loves its tentacular creatures, its octopodes and squid-monsters, who represent a monstrous alterity, an otherness, which is quite distinct from the fundamentally humanoid monsters we will encounter in Chapter 1, or the human-animal metamorphoses of Chapter 3. The weird, Fisher proposes, 'is that *which does not belong*'. Does not belong, that is, within our very narrow perception and conception of reality. If the uncanny is unsettling because it allows us a momentary peep through a crack in the doors of perception, the weird blows those doors apart. An encounter with the weird is terrifying because it can completely remove the foundations on which we base reality.

Popular Anxieties

Horror is an embodied art form; but it is also, and at the same time, a cultural one. While, I have suggested, it has its origins inscribed into the very beginnings of the Western literary and cultural tradition, it comes down to us today primarily as a *popular cultural* form, in pulp fiction, in film, and increasingly in video games and online.

'Popular culture' is a highly disputed term. Following the work of the so-called Frankfurt School of cultural studies, and most particularly of the philosopher Theodor Adorno in *The Culture Industry* and elsewhere, some commentators view popular culture as a medium through which hegemony enforces its values. It is entertainment which does the thinking for its audience, presenting them with cultural forms which he notoriously likened to pre-digested baby food. In a brilliant modern adaptation of Adorno, Curtis White understands contemporary popular culture as productive of a bland, conformist 'middle mind', incapable of critique and resisting spontaneity and authenticity. Influenced by the work of Stuart Hall and others, some British theorists of popular culture view it as, in John Storey's words, 'a site of struggle between the "resistance" of subordinate groups in society and the forces of "incorporation" operating in the interests of dominant groups in society'. Recently, and more blithely, in a specifically British context the historian Dominic Sandbrook understands popular culture as the authentic expression of the modern spirit of the nation.

Horror is a phobic cultural form. Some theories of horror see it as addressing 'our deepest fears', essentially static, part of a fundamentally unchanging 'human condition'. But our fears are not fixed; they are mutable and contingent, a product of historical context. In his influential study, *Sociophobics*, the cultural anthropologist David L. Scruton writes: 'Fearing is an event that takes place in a social setting; it is performed by social animals whose lives and experiences are dominated by culture.... Fearing is thus a dimension of human social life.'

As I have already argued, the origins of horror are inextricably a part of human civilization. But this does not mean that our fears are always the same. One of the most famous of all definitions of horror falls into the 'our deepest fears' category, and is often cited as axiomatic. In 1927, H. P. Lovecraft published 'Supernatural Horror in Literature', a critical essay which was the culmination of his deep, if idiosyncratic, engagement with his chosen literary form. Lovecraft begins with these famous words: 'The oldest and strongest emotion of mankind is fear, and the oldest and strongest kind of fear is fear of the unknown.' This is an appealing formulation, and intuitively it makes a lot of sense. No one would deny that 'fear of the unknown' is potent, and an important part of the power of horror. Yet as a totalizing definition, it is clearly partial, and in some cases demonstrably wrong.

One of the characteristics of popular culture is its speed and suppleness (which some have dismissed as its ephemerality or disposability): the ways in which it is able to provide an instant response to events, developments, moods, crises. These responses are often inchoate, not thought through. Popular culture tends to identify, finger, and probe issues and anxieties, rather than provide coherent answers.

A good example of this would be to look at the year 1897. This was Queen Victoria's Diamond Jubilee, and might fairly be said to represent the high-water mark of the British Empire. Yet any reader of the popular fiction of the period would have seen that beneath the public assertiveness of British imperialism, the anxieties were showing. Colonial horror, in which British relations with its imperial Others

Introduction

became Gothicized in narratives of magic, monstrosity, and revenge, became enormously popular in the last decades of the nineteenth century. Some of its foremost proponents were writers whose imperial connections were very powerful.

Rudyard Kipling is perhaps the greatest of all writers of the British Empire. His story 'The Mark of the Beast' is the tale of a colonial administrator who violates a Hindu altar and is cursed with a form of lycanthropy. The story has as its epigraph a 'Native Proverb', 'Your Gods and my Gods—do you or I know which are the stronger?', and opens with a revealingly relativistic theological statement:

East of Suez, some hold, the direct control of Providence ceases; Man being there handed over to the power of the Gods and Devils of Asia, and the Church of England Providence only exercising an occasional and modified supervision in the case of Englishmen.

The vengeful 'power of the Gods and Devils of Asia', or of Africa, a discourse of uneasy Orientalism, pervades much British imperial fiction.

'I am an Imperialist', Arthur Conan Doyle wrote to the *Irish Times* in 1912, 'because I believe the whole to be greater than the part, and I would always willingly sacrifice any part if I thought it to the advantage of the whole.' Doyle's many public pronouncements on the British Empire, for example in his histories of the Boer War and the First World War, were on occasion downright jingoistic in tone and sentiment. And yet a recurring trope in Doyle's fiction—from Sherlock Holmes stories such as *The Sign of the Four* or 'The Speckled Band' to Gothic tales such as 'Uncle Jeremy's

23

Household', 'The Brazilian Cat', or 'The Brown Hand'—is that of the vengeful subjects or monsters of Empire who loom out of the darkness to torment the British.

These tales are fictional explorations of the common *fin-de-siècle* cultural anxiety of reverse colonization, which saw a series of continental, oriental, imperial, or interplanetary Others wreaking havoc upon British soil. Thus, to return to 1897, it is no accident that this imperial zenith also saw the publication of three of the defining works of reverse colonization: Bram Stoker's *Dracula*, Richard Marsh's Egyptomaniac classic *The Beetle*, and (in serial form) H. G. Wells's *The War of the Worlds*. In all these works, the British Empire is shown as vulnerable not only to attack, but to an attack on its very heart, as these monstrous invaders head straight for the imperial metropolis of London. Works such as these, then, are not (or not primarily) comments on 'our deepest fears', or on fear of the unknown, but arise out of, and give form to, social and political anxieties of the 1890s.

For my own generation (I was born in 1967), the great anxiety was nuclear holocaust. Coming of age in the Reagan–Thatcher 1980s, we witnessed a number of historical events and cultural products all tending to increase our sense of awareness and terror: Three Mile Island, Chernobyl, Greenham Common, *When the Wind Blows*, *Threads*, 'Protect and Survive', *War Games*, *Edge of Darkness*, *Terminator 2*. This was an utterly new terror for humanity—the possibility, for the first time in human history, not of individual death or even of species extinction, but of total world annihilation. When Edward Teller and his team first tested the hydrogen bomb in the 1950s, there was a real possibility that the explosion caused would set off a chain reaction which would ignite the entire earth's atmosphere. They did it anyway. For many, the knowledge of nuclear Armageddon was existentially unbearable. Famously, on receiving the Nobel Prize in Literature on 10 December 1950, William Faulkner said: 'our tragedy today is a general and universal physical fear so long sustained by now that we can even bear it. There are no longer problems of the spirit. There is only the question: "When will I be blown up?"' Stephen King, steeped in postwar American history and popular culture, made the same point in 1981:

> We were fertile ground for the seeds of terror, we war babies; we had been raised in a strange circus atmosphere of para- noia, patriotism, and national *hubris*. We were told that we were the greatest nation on earth and that any Iron Curtain outlaw who tried to draw down on us in that great saloon of international politics would discover who the fastest gun in the West was . . . but we were also told exactly what to keep in our fallout shelters and how long we would have to stay in there after we won the war. We had more to eat than any other nation in the history of the world, but there were traces of Strontium-90 in our milk from nuclear testing.

The problem with nuclear anxieties was not that these fears were unknown, but that we knew *exactly* what to be afraid of. Any viewer of *Threads* (1984), which dealt with the aftermath of a nuclear attack on the British city of Sheffield, would have witnessed not only the initial megadeaths from the blast itself, but then the ravages of radiation sickness, nuclear winter, resource scarcity, and social breakdown. In 1985, the BBC repeated *Threads* the day after it broadcast its long-suppressed 1965 precursor, *The War Game*. Cumulatively, these two nights were among the most terrifying experiences of my life.

As Cormac McCarthy's *The Road* (2006) shows, these nuclear anxieties have certainly not disappeared altogether. Indeed, one can detect them in displaced form in the post-millennial wave of zombie narratives, from *28 Days Later* (2002) to *The Walking Dead* (first broadcast 2010), and much else besides. And yet, unlike the Baby Boomers and Generation Xers before them, contemporary Millennials do not seem to lie awake at night as I did, dreading the appearance of a mushroom cloud on the horizon. Aldermaston and Greenham Common are historical terms, if not meaningless ones.

But the bombs have not gone away; the world can still be destroyed many times over. It is fear—cultural anxiety—that has moved, taken new forms. Contemporary fears of global warming and ecological catastrophe have produced a post-millennial wave of ecohorrors, as we shall see in the Afterword, and a formidable body of scholarly and theoretical work has grown quickly in response.

For equally obvious reasons, the last years have seen the arrival of a new subgenre of digital horror. Levan Gabriadze's startling *Unfriended* (2014), about a vengeful supernatural social media stalker, for example, speaks directly to a generation of viewers who have lived their entire lives online, and for whom digital social networks may be more vividly and urgently real than the lived experience of human communities. More than this, though, what is disturbing about *Unfriended* is its analysis of online life as an existential habit of being, or even a morbid addiction. For the characters of *Unfriended*, logging out of digital social networks is manifestly impossible, or even literally inconceivable. While, with its teens-in-peril narrative, the film structurally resembles 1980s slasher movies, and also clearly draws on the 1990s and early 2000s cycle of supernatural retribution films such as *Ring* (1998) or *Final Destination* (2000), the locus of the film's anxiety is entirely contemporary: the impossibility of a meaningful life offline.

It falls upon each generation, then, to create its own monsters, or at least its own unique iterations of monstrosity. There is a good reason why vampires cast no reflections in the mirror. It is because what looks back at us is ourselves. We invest in monsters our own anxieties, but also sometimes our own desires, inarticulable in respectable social discourse. Monsters body forth our dreams and our nightmares, and they are the subject of my first chapter.

1

Monsters

'Understand death?' Stephen King writes, from the perspective of his child protagonist Mark Petrie in his vampire novel *'Salem's Lot* (1975). 'Sure. That was when the monsters got you.' Central to the power of horror is the spectacle of the monster. 'Monster' may, in fact, etymologically be connected to 'spectacle', or something very close: 'demonstrate', from the Latin *monstrare*, to show; 'monster', from *monstrum*, portent or atrocity (that which reveals), which can be traced back etymologically to *monere*, to warn. So, a monster can be simultaneously a spectacle, an atrocity (or violation), and a warning, an omen, or a punishment.

It makes sense, then, to begin our analysis of horror with some of its monsters. In this chapter we will be looking particularly at two of the most widely circulated types of monster, the vampire and the zombie. Why are we so fascinated by these figures? What do they mean?

The answer is that they mean many things, or have meant many things, across the centuries, as we shall see. Monstrosity is a physical category, describing the limit-points of the fleshly mutability we discussed in the Introduction. Historically, for example, it has been used to describe extreme deformity, from specimens of two-headed births to conjoined twins, lepers, or the hydrocephalic. But it is also a cultural, moral, or political category. 'Monstrous' births could be understood as omens. Here is the fourteenth-century Monk Thomas Burton of Meaux Abbey in Yorkshire, writing about one such 'monster', whose birth portended the arrival of the black death:

> And shortly before this time, there was a certain human monster in England, divided from the navel upwards and both masculine and feminine, and joined in the lower part. When one part ate, drank, slept or spoke, the other could do something else if it wished. One died before the other, and the survivor held it in its arms for three days. They used to sing together very sweetly. They died, aged about 18, at Kingston upon Hull a short time before the pestilence began.

Typically, Burton's 'certain human monster'—a pair of conjoined twins—cuts across a number of stable conceptual categories: both two and one, male and female, and in the end both living and dead.

The fabulous monsters of bestiaries, from Pliny the Elder's *Natural History* (*c*.77–79 AD) onwards—the manticore, the gorgon, the gryphon, the basilisk, the chimaera—are generally made up of fanciful combinations of known animals. The manticore, for example, has the body of a lion and the head of a man, and sometimes the tail of a scorpion, while the chimaera is a lion with a goat's head growing out of its back. Typically, these monsters were encountered in far-flung lands by travellers or military campaigners. Classically, monstrosity rarely inhabits the household—when it does arrive at home, it comes as a dread warning or portent, or as a punishment for sins. Monstrosity makes its home in exotic climes, far from centres of civilization and modernity: Skull Island, the Land that Time Forgot, Castle Dracula. This is what I meant when I said that monstrosity could be a political category. It can arise out of the body of thinking that Edward Said has called Orientalism—a tendency to understand the non-European as an inhuman Other, as bestial, cruel, sensuous. The logic of Orientalism has often been used as a justificatory mechanism for colonialism, conquest, and enslavement.

Contemporary modernity seems particularly obsessed by the monsters that consume us, that eat our flesh or drink our blood, to the extent that we might seem to be obsessed by our own consumption, or to welcome it. Social and individual behaviour is governed and regulated, we have seen, by powerful systems of taboos. In the Introduction, I argued that horror is an intrinsic feature of human civilization, and is intimately connected to the concept of taboo—to systems of regulation and proscription, interdict and abomination, which, it has been argued, are at the very root of human culture.

Taboo, Freud believed, is 'the oldest human unwritten code of laws. It is generally supposed that taboo is older than gods and dates back to a period before any kind of religion existed.' One of the strongest sets of taboos surrounds food, eating, and culinary practices, and so allegations of various forms of 'unclean eating' are often a way of marking out non-humanity. The most widespread of these food taboos is the taboo against cannibalism, and our bestiaries, romances, and mythologies provide a rich history of man-eating monsters, from Kronos devouring his children, to the Cyclops gorging on Odysseus' men, to any number of ogres, giants, trolls, and corpse-eating ghouls.

It should not surprise us that the history of European colonial encounters has in part been written as a history of encounters with cannibals. As his name suggests, *The Tempest*'s Caliban, the aboriginal native of Prospero's island, is one such cannibal. The word 'cannibal', in fact, derives from 'Carib', the people of the Antilles in what is now the West Indies—thus, the Caribbean Sea is, etymologically at least, the Sea of Cannibals. When early modern European explorers first encountered the Caribs in the sixteenth century, this is what they claimed to have encountered. However, even some contemporaries were sceptical. The great essayist Michel de Montaigne's celebrated 'On Cannibals' reads today like an early example of cultural relativism, or even of postcolonial political writing:

> I do not believe, from what I have been told about this people [the Caribs], that there is anything barbarous or savage about them, except that we call barbarous anything that is contrary to our own habits....We are justified therefore in calling these people barbarians by reference to the laws of reason, but not in comparison with ourselves, who surpass them in every kind of barbarity.

Since the publication of William Arens's *The Man-Eating Myth* in 1979, there has been a vigorous debate among anthropologists, historians, and literary scholars as to whether, or to what degree, or under what circumstances, human societies have systematically practised cannibalism. A modern tradition of liberal, culturally relativistic anthropological thinking understands this systematic or ritualistic cannibalism as essentially a racist myth, a justifying projection of the colonial mind.

But the imagination of horror has seized on the possibilities of cannibalism. Nineteenth-century maritime and colonial horror, from Edgar Allan Poe's *The Narrative of Arthur Gordon Pym of Nantucket* to Herman Melville's *Moby-Dick* to H. G. Wells's *The Island of Doctor Moreau* to Joseph Conrad's *Heart of Darkness*, is fascinated by cannibalism. *Cannibal Holocaust* and its ilk, the Italian cannibal movies of the 'video nasty' era which we looked at in the Introduction, are justifiably notorious for the outrageous viscerality of their images, but what is really troubling to me about these films is their racism, the casual cultural brutality with which they subhumanize Amazonian tribes. Scarcely less shocking, but rather more nuanced, the redneck and hillbilly cannibal families of Tobe Hooper's *The Texas Chain Saw Massacre* (1974) or Wes Craven's *The Hills Have Eyes* (1977) offer domestic American versions of the colonial cannibal Other, albeit that these films also have serious observations to make about the cultural marginalization and economic disenfranchisement of regional America, issues which remain current to this day.

Conversely, our most celebrated contemporary cannibal, Dr Hannibal Lecter, acts not out of a sense of cultural and economic disenfranchisement, but rather (like certain vampires) out of a sense of superiority. Thomas Harris's Baltimore Renaissance Man is variously *gourmand*, psychiatrist, anatomist, artist, musician, orientalist, historian of high culture, patron of the arts, serial killer, cannibal, and demon. In Harris's prequel novel, *Hannibal Rising* (2006), a policeman muses on the young Lecter: 'What is he now? There's not a word for it yet. For lack of a better word, we'll call him a monster.'

For a writer, reader, or viewer in the first decades of the twenty-first century, monsters have become an inescapable presence in popular culture, from whom there seems to be nowhere to run. 'We live', to quote an influential commentator on the subject, 'in a time of monsters.' There have been numerous books and PhD theses written, for example, on the phenomenon of contemporary vampire culture. A whole industry has emerged in critical and scholarly commentary, in academic conferences, learned articles, and on the blogosphere, providing often highly sophisticated analyses of developments in horror almost as quickly as the culture industry can produce them. This might be seen as part of a widespread acceleration of culture, producing and responding to a bewildering new technological and political landscape. This has perhaps understandably led one 2013 book on *Monster Culture in the 21st Century* to propose that 'over the past decade we have been terrorized by change', and that consequently 'monstrosity has transcended its status as metaphor and has indeed become a necessary condition for our existence in the twenty-first century'. Monsters, the authors suggest, have become a means of managing contemporary threats, crises, and anxieties. At the very least, I believe, they have become a means by which we can think through the contemporary situation.

The literary critic Nina Auerbach once suggested that vampires are like immigrants, in that viewed from afar, or through the eyes of ignorance, they all look alike, but once you get close up what is most striking about them is their differences, their multiplicity. Béla Lugosi would probably consider Robert Pattinson an intolerable wimp. The zombies who worked sugar plantations and the zombies who devour human flesh at the end of civilization both understand economic exploitation, but wouldn't agree on shared means, let alone shared meals. The King Kong of 1933 and the King Kong of 2017 may both emerge from periods of economic depression, but they have very different stories to tell. As we have seen, Hannibal Lecter and *The Texas Chain Saw Massacre*'s Sawyer family don't really move in the same social circles at all.

Vampires

The vampire is the iconic monster of modern horror. Vampires refuse to go away, though they may go underground for periods, and are easily the most widespread and influential of all horror monsters, capable of startling acts of reinvention. Although, as Paul Barber very convincingly argues in *Vampires, Burial and Death*, the origins of the vampire may well lie in the folkloric attempts of the pre-modern mind to understand the physical processes of death, it appears to be the case that in the figure of the bloodsucking undead, modernity seems to have found its great all-purpose metaphor, capable of speaking to successive generations on their own terms.

The extraordinary popularity of Stephenie Meyer's *Twilight* series of books and films, aimed squarely at a young teen audience, suggests a number of intersecting phenomena: adolescent sexuality, romanticism, and a sense of outsiderliness; religious sensibilities (some commentators read *Twilight* as emanating directly from Meyer's Mormonism); the power of marketing, corporatization, and celebrity culture; varieties of new media (*Twilight* gave birth to the *Fifty Shades of Grey* series, which began life as online *Twilight* fan fiction); the sense of a kind of accelerated generational slippage and perpetual youth culture (the 'Twi-Mom' phenomenon, in which mothers appropriated their daughters' cultural tastes). The success of *Twilight* has led to other, similar ventures, such as the *Vampire Diaries* young adult fiction and TV series, or the Sookie Stackhouse *Southern Vampire Mysteries/True Blood* cycle of books and TV series, aimed at a slightly older audience (the Stackhouse novels actually predate *Twilight*, but the success of *True Blood* is clearly a response to the phenomenon). The *Twilight* phenomenon has defined the terms by which twenty-first-century vampires are understood. When Neil Jordan's *Byzantium*, for example, was released in cinemas in 2013, around the time the *Twilight* series was reaching its cinematic climax, it was referred to (or virally marketed) as 'the other *Twilight*', or 'the alternative to *Twilight*'.

But vampires have not always embodied youth and its glamour: this is a distinctively modern twist, which in essence dates to the publication of Anne Rice's *Interview with the Vampire* (1976). This section of the chapter will look at the vampire's history, from its beginnings in European folklore as an undead revenant (usually a peasant) returning from the grave to prey on relatives and fellow villagers, generally taken to represent a pre-modern means of understanding plague by blaming death upon the dead.

In parts of early modern Europe, vampires were a fact of life. Periodically, the dead returned, rising from their graves to prey upon the living. The causes of infection and disease were fundamentally mysterious until the formulation of the germ theory of disease in the second half of the nineteenth century. The natural decomposition processes of the human body were poorly understood—due to the build-up of gases, for example, corpses can be astonishingly buoyant, often seemingly disinterring themselves if not buried deeply enough, or if water tables rose. Under some conditions, corpses needed to be staked into the earth to prevent this from happening. Vampires, then, were originally an imaginative means to understand pestilence and death, providing a supernatural explanation for incomprehensible natural processes. At times of plague, the sheer number of dead bodies made burial difficult—the dead seemed to be bursting out of shallow graves, poisoning water supplies, visiting the living at night, preying upon them.

These vampire epidemics afflicted Europe until as late as the eighteenth century. The much-discussed case of the Serbian vampire Arnold Paole, who died shortly after returning from military service in Turkey in 1727, only seemingly to rise from the grave and prey on his home village, was the subject of an official legal investigation. Its report, *Visum et Repertum* (*Seen and Destroyed*), concluded that Paole was indeed a vampire, and ordered that his victims be disinterred, beheaded, and burnt, and their ashes scattered into the river (a boundary of running water which vampires were believed to be unable to cross). In 1746, the Benedictine scholar Augustine Calmet published a lengthy and high-profile treatise on vampirism, which was translated into English as *The Phantom World*, and was commented upon by a variety of contemporary figures, including Pope Benedict XIV (whose position on the existence of vampires was equivocal). For Enlightenment figures such as Diderot and Voltaire, a belief in vampires could only arise from the superstition and credulity they saw as their mission to correct. Rousseau understood them as emblematic of the contradictions inherent in traditional judicial, military, medical, and ecclesiastical authority, and thus of orders of power undermining themselves: 'No evidence is lacking—depositions, certificates of notables, surgeons, priests and magistrates. The proof *in law* is utterly complete. . . . Yet with all this, who actually *believes* in vampires?'

Though unquestionably revenants, 'folkloric' vampires such as Arnold Paole and his ilk tend to be peasants or rural villagers, intensely localized in their effects. In appearance, they are often described as ruddy faced, as though bloated with blood. How did we get from these frankly unsexy undead yokels to the characteristic vampire of modern popular culture—suave, aristocratic, cultivated, pale, and desirable?

This vampire is a distinctive product of the literary culture of Romanticism. As the critic Mario Praz identified as long ago as 1933, there is a recurring strain of 'Dark Romanticism' which is fascinated by the allure of supernatural and demonic creatures (Lamia, Geraldine, and other serpent-women, Life-in-Death, La Belle Dame Sans Merci) and by human transgressors and overreachers standing apart from the common concerns of humanity (Faust, Frankenstein, Napoleon). In April 1819, the *New Monthly Magazine* published a tale entitled *The Vampyre*, whose protagonist, the charismatic and seductive Lord Ruthven, returns to London from his

European Grand Tour, having died in Greece and arisen as a vampire. Published anonymously, the work was assumed to be by Lord Byron (Goethe thought it among his best work), though it was in fact written by the Edinburgh physician Dr John Polidori. Polidori was present at the evening of supernatural tales told at the Villa Diodati on the shores of Lake Geneva in 1816 which was the genesis of Mary Shelley's *Frankenstein*. Told as they have been from a variety of different and differing sources, the events of this evening are difficult to reconstruct with certainty, but it seems likely that Polidori based *The Vampyre* on the supernatural tale which Byron himself told that night (a fragment of which was subsequently published), and drew heavily on the scandalous public persona of Byron himself for Lord Ruthven.

With Romantic writers such as Byron and Polidori, the vampire became, importantly, both sexualized and aristocratic, a demon lover, running riot across the poetry, fiction, and theatre of the nineteenth century right up to the publication of the single most important text in the history of horror, Bram Stoker's *Dracula*, in 1897. At the same time, Karl Marx habitually deployed the vampire as a metaphor for the 'bloodsucking' economic exploitation of capitalism (one wonders what he would have made of the *Twilight* phenomenon, capitalism red in fang and claw?). Marx was much given to Gothic metaphors, and when casting around in *Capital* (1867) for an exemplar of 'The Voracious Appetite for Surplus Labour', settles on 'a Wallachian Boyar...in the Danubian Principalities' (was he thinking of Vlad the Impaler?). A couple of pages earlier, Marx offers his celebrated account of bloodsucking capitalism:

> [The] capitalist...is only capital personified. His soul is the soul of capital. But capital has one sole driving force, the drive to valorize itself, to create surplus-value, to make its constant part, the means of production, absorb the greatest possible amount of surplus labour. Capital is dead labour which, vampire-like, lives only by sucking living labour, and lives the more, the more labour it sucks.

The class polarities of vampirism have been reversed. Marx's vampiric 'Wallachian Boyar' exploits the labour of the very people (the Eastern European poor) who were traditionally prone to vampirism.

What this demonstrates is that, by the mid-nineteenth century, vampirism had infected the cultural bloodstream, where it has remained ever since. (Our vampires are figures of speech, put to a variety of uses.) In popular culture, James Malcolm Rymer's 'penny blood' behemoth *Varney the Vampire* (1845–7) found in its immortal undead protagonist the perfect vehicle for a potentially endlessly recyclable plot. Sir Francis Varney is killed many times, by almost all means imaginable, but can always be resurrected by exposure to moonlight (a favourite nineteenth-century vampiric restorative)—until, finally consumed by self-disgust, and at the demand of the publisher, Edward Lloyd, he flings himself into Vesuvius, where the moon never shines. The demands of the market can kill off seemingly indestructible monsters, but they can also bring them back at any time.

Vampires also enjoyed a lively undeath onstage across the course of the century. Charles Nodier's adaptation of Polidori, *Le Vampire*, was a huge hit on the Parisian stage in

1820, and led to a craze for vampire plays in the city. One contemporary critic wrote: 'There is not a theatre in Paris without its Vampire! At the Porte-Saint-Martin we have *Le Vampire*; at the Vaudeville *Le Vampire* again; at the Varieties *Les Trois Vampires ou le clair de la lune*.' Nodier's play was immediately adapted into English by James Robinson Planché, whose play *The Vampire, or The Bride of the Isles* opened in London's Lyceum in August 1820, and introduced a sensational new stage device: an onstage trapdoor which allowed the actors seemingly to disappear, accompanied by a puff of smoke. This trapdoor was, and still is, called a 'vampire'. In the 1850s, the celebrated Dublin dramatist Dion Boucicault resurrected Polidori again for productions in London (*The Vampire*) and New York (*The Phantom*).

In 1872, another Dubliner, Joseph Sheridan Le Fanu, published the novella 'Carmilla' as part of his portmanteau collection *In a Glass Darkly*. 'Carmilla' has had an enormous influence on subsequent vampire culture because of its dreamlike narrative logic, its remote Central European gentry class setting, and most particularly its exploration of the homoerotics of vampirism. Laura, the young female narrator, recalls her troubling and yet exciting relationship with the vampire Carmilla:

> Sometimes after an hour of apathy, my strange and beautiful companion would take my hand and hold it with a fond pressure, renewed again and again; blushing softly, gazing in my face with languid and burning eyes, and breathing so fast that her dress rose and fell with the tumultuous respiration. It was like the ardour of a lover; it embarrassed

> me; it was hateful and yet overpowering; and with gloating
> eyes she drew me to her, and her hot lips travelled along my
> cheek in kisses, and she would whisper, almost in sobs, 'You
> are mine, you *shall be mine*, you and I are one forever.'

Our relationship to our monsters is a dialectical one—we are, simultaneously, irresistibly drawn to them (we can't take our eyes off them) and revolted by them (they disgust us). More precisely, the strength of our attraction to them disgusts us, and yet the more we are repulsed by monsters, the stronger our desire for them. In *Totem and Taboo*, Freud describes the concept of taboo as characterized by 'emotional ambivalence': 'The meaning of "taboo", as we see it, diverges in two contrasting directions. To us it means, on the one hand, "sacred", "consecrated", and on the other "uncanny", "dangerous", "forbidden", "unclean".' Taboos are powerful because they are called on to regulate potentially overwhelming desires. 'I was conscious of a love growing into adoration, and also of abhorrence', Laura admits. Carmilla's bite is intensely sexual: 'Sometimes it was as if warm lips kissed me, and longer and more lovingly as they reached my throat, but there the caress fixed itself.' In *Dracula*, Jonathan Harker, face to face with the Count's vampire brides, responds with the same 'emotional ambivalence' of desire and repulsion:

> All three had brilliant white teeth, that shone like pearls
> against the ruby of their voluptuous lips. There was some-
> thing about them that made me uneasy, some longing and
> at the same time some deadly fear. I felt in my heart a
> wicked, burning desire that they should kiss me with those
> red lips.

Bleeding over boundaries, the vampire's red, fanged mouth is an archetypal image of horror and anxiety. It is Eros and Thanatos, desire and death, consumption and abjection; it is both male and female; it penetrates and encloses; it is the *vagina dentata*.

Bram Stoker's great novel is a rich and complex work. It is, first of all, one of the major novels of Victorian London. Reading *Dracula*, we encounter a city of immigrants and suburbs, gentlemen's clubs, lawyers, banks, docks, graveyards, and lunatic asylums. The novel's zoophagous lunatic, R. M. Renfield, is an unclean eater who plans to consume his way up a chain of being, from flies to spiders to birds to cats, presumably ending with cannibalism. Once a high-ranking member of the Windham, one of London's most exclusive gentlemen's clubs, Renfield is an insane establishmentarian Englishman, now completely in thrall to the Count, a dangerously exotic foreigner who carries with him disease, dirt, and infection which will enter the English bloodstream.

One of the first things we discover about the Count is his unbearable stench: 'As the Count leaned over me and his hands touched me, I could not repress a shudder. It may have been that his breath was rank, but a horrible feeling of nausea came over me which, do what I would, I could not conceal.' In Castle Dracula, the Count's lair is 'an old, ruined chapel, which had evidently been used as a graveyard', which Harker enters through 'a tunnel-like passage, through which came a deathly, sickly odour, the odour of old earth newly turned. As I went through the passage, the smell grew closer and heavier.' In London, Dracula hides out in the ruined chapel of Carfax Abbey, where the stench is worse still, intensified commensurate with the size of the city:

> There was an earthy smell, as of some dry miasma, which came through the fouler air. But as to the odour itself, how shall I describe it? It was not alone that it was composed of all the ills of mortality and with the pungent, acrid smell of blood, but it seemed as though corruption had become itself corrupt. Faugh! It sickens me to think of it. Every breath exhaled by that monster seemed to have clung to the place and intensified its loathsomeness.... We all instinctively drew back. The whole place was becoming alive with rats.... The rats were multiplying in their thousands, and we moved out.

Dracula, as we have seen, is one of a number of reverse colonization narratives published in and around the year 1897. In this novel, the British Empire is vulnerable to invasion and infection, a permeable membrane, like skin easily punctured by the vampire's kiss.

But even in 1897, the real future of vampires was on the screen, not the page or the stage. In Francis Ford Coppola's celebrated 1992 adaptation of *Dracula*, Gary Oldman's count— suave and debonair, rejuvenated by his contact with the modern city of London—goes to see the Lumière Brothers' Cinematograph, up-to-the-minute technology first unveiled in 1895. In 1896, the writer Maxim Gorky responded in horror to a Cinematograph showing in Moscow, believing he had had an encounter with the undead:

> Your nerves are strained, imagination carries you to some unnaturally monotonous life, a life without colour and without sound, but full of movement, the life of ghosts, or of people, *damned* to the damnation of eternal silence, people who have been deprived of all the colours of life.

Vampires and their close counterparts played an important role in early cinema. There is something *spectral* about the experience of cinema, as Gorky understood: to enter the cinema is to cross a boundary, a threshold into the supernatural world. 'And when he had crossed the bridge, the phantoms came to meet him', reads a haunting intertitle from *Nosferatu: Ein Symphonie des Grauens* (*Nosferatu: A Symphony of Horror*), F. W. Murnau's free, unauthorized 1922 adaptation of *Dracula*. The extraordinary aesthetics of German expressionist cinema, which made manifest the symbolic possibilities of shadow and shape in a world 'without colour and without sound', were brilliantly suited to represent the land of phantoms, out of which they seemed to have emerged (Figure 2). The artist and occultist Albin Grau was responsible for *Nosferatu*'s unforgettable production and set design, and in the uncanny person of Max Schreck's Graf Orlok, the film offers a vampire utterly removed from human sympathy and concerns. With his pointed ears and fanged incisors, Orlok is a rat in (near-)human form, and a plague of rats accompanies him when he disembarks a ship in Wisborg, bringing disease to the town.

While sound came to cinema in 1929, early vampire films still tended to use it sparingly, as though acknowledging that naturalistic dialogue, in particular, would break the spell. Carl Dreyer's beautiful, dreamlike *Vampyr* (1933) is a *very* free, imagistic adaptation of 'Carmilla', largely silent. A much more straightforward film, Tod Browning's *Dracula* (1931), is again punctuated by long silences. Subsequent popular culture would have been very different without the iconic performance of the great Hungarian actor Béla

Figure 2. Albin Grau, poster for *Nosferatu* (1922).

Lugosi in the title role of this film. Lugosi definitively established the dominant iconography of the screen vampire—
the widow's peak, the evening dress, the opera cape, the

mannered delivery (Lugosi spoke little English in 1931, and had to learn his lines phonetically).

The monochrome world of Browning and of the Universal Studios horror stable, with their roots in German expressionist cinema, in vaudeville and carnival, and in stage melodrama, established a paradigm for horror cinema which was to remain dominant until the first horror releases of Hammer Studios in the mid-1950s. A low-budget independent studio, Hammer operated effectively as a repertory company of actors, directors, and technicians, recycling plots, costumes, and locations often to ingenious effect. Arising out of the bleak and straitened post-war British world of bombsites and urban redevelopment, national service, and scarcity and (until 1954) ration cards, Hammer clearly offered a fantasy alternative. Engaged in a constant running battle with the British censors, Hammer's was a highly sexualized world, heightened by a lurid primary-colour palette particularly characterized by the liberal use of the deep red cinematic fake blood known as Kensington Gore, quantities of which were often smeared over the fanged mouth of the imperious, magnetic Christopher Lee.

It is difficult to overestimate how modern Hammer's sensibilities must have seemed when *Dracula* was released in 1957, but by the time Lee hung up his cape after *The Satanic Rites of Dracula* in 1973, the studio's output seemed stale and out of touch, formally and ideologically conservative. Two years later, vampires definitively entered the contemporary world, where they have remained ever since. Stephen King's *'Salem's Lot* (1975) exchanged Transylvania, Styria, or Victorian London for a recognizably downbeat New England small town, and was, like all its author's works, steeped in post-war American popular culture—its literary frame of reference was not the Gothic canon of Le Fanu and Stoker but rather the works of the writers which King and his generation grew up reading—Shirley Jackson, Ray Bradbury, and Richard Matheson, whose apocalyptic vampire-zombie classic *I Am Legend* (1954) is an early example of a distinctive American pop-cultural interpretation of traditional Gothic monsters. *'Salem's Lot*, in fact, enacts a clash between the aristocratic Old European vampire Kurt Barlow—who comes to New England along with his suave henchman Straker in the guise of a pair of gay antiques dealers, selling 'old things, fine things'— and the contemporary American world of rock music, television, Vietnam, and Richard Nixon. Barlow is eventually destroyed by King's characteristic combination of a writer and a child, but not before spawning a new breed of distinctively American vampires, democratic, demotic, proudly vulgar.

None of these are terms that would apply to Anne Rice's vampires. Rice's *Interview with the Vampire* was published in 1976, the year after *'Salem's Lot*, and has proved no less influential. Rice's ancient vampires clearly understand themselves as the custodians of Western high culture—they are vastly wealthy, aesthetes, commodity fetishists, and acquisitors. Whether uncanny, abject, exotic, or aristocratic, vampires before Rice had tended to be distinctively Other. Stoker's Count Dracula gives fascinating glimpses into his history at the beginning of the novel, and then effectively disappears from his own narrative, an invisible terror to be prevented at all costs. For Rice, vampirism is an aspirational condition, and it has largely remained so ever since, as the vampire has become a major figure in the popular subcategory of horror known as Paranormal Romance. Her readers don't want to kill vampires; they want to *be* them. After Rice, vampires have a rich interiority that amounts to utter self-absorption. They have their needs and desires, their losses and longings; they deserve not our fear or our hatred, but our sympathy, our envy, even our love. While some contemporary vampires often go to ingenious lengths to avoid killing innocent people (they prey on animals, they visit blood banks, they only drink the blood of criminals or the wicked), I think we should nevertheless be troubled by a vampire culture which aspires to the condition of understanding humanity as an inferior species.

Zombies

On 23 July 2011, an estimated 8,000 people gathered in St Stephen's Green in the centre of my home city of Dublin for an extraordinary event. This was the annual 'zombie walk', in which members of the public parade through the city dressed as the living dead, often with extraordinarily inventive make-up—white, grey, green, or blue faces; generous deployment of 'Kensington gore'; torn or missing bits of flesh, sometimes with teeth visible through holes in the cheek or jaw; sunken, hollow, blacked out, or even missing eyes, or eyeballs dangling out of their sockets; shabby, torn clothing—often formal suits in a state of some distress (Figure 3). Some of them appear to be munching on what look disturbingly like severed human limbs. And then—they *shamble*. Thousands of them, shambling through the city centre, an army of the risen dead on the march, *coming to get you!*

49

Figure 3. Brains! A Dublin zombie walker.

Dublin isn't the only city to stage an annual zombie walk, nor was it the first; and its walk is certainly not the largest. It appears that the first ever zombie walk was staged, semi-spontaneously, in a gamers' convention in Milwaukee in 2000. This, you might think, is just the kind of thing that Midwestern computer gamers might get up to, being semi-socialized nerds who need to get a life. But it's not that simple. The idea soon caught on, and cities all over the US, and then all over the world, began to witness these out-breaks, as if the zombie apocalypse which films, TV, comics, and games had warned us about for the last few decades had finally arrived.

Why would people do this? The thousands of people who gather annually for these events are not all computer nerds with no friends, nor are they all hirsute adolescents with impressive collections of death metal records (and no friends). But they are mostly young people, and largely highly educated—students and youngish college graduates in their twenties and early thirties, with a fair representation of high-school kids among them too. What drives these members of the young urban bourgeoisie to gather together in these enormous flash mobs, a parade of the walking dead?

There are many answers, but one of them—and for me the most significant—is political. It's no accident that these outbreaks of zombification have greatly intensified across Western cities since the global financial crash of 2008. Perhaps unconsciously to themselves, the zombie walkers are *protesting*.

If vampires, at least after Romanticism, have tended to be aristocratic individualists, feared and admired as a 'superior' adaptation of humanity, then zombies are a monstrous underclass, an undifferentiated, mindless *lumpenproletarian* mass. Though its origins are to be found in African religion, the figure of the zombie is most closely associated with the Caribbean, and particularly with Haitian voodoo beliefs. In voodoo, the zombie is a body returned from the dead by a sorcerer, completely devoid of will, there to do the sorcerer's bidding. When the writer and ethnographer Zora Neale Hurston visited Haiti in 1936–7, she began to hear stories of zombies, and particularly the case of Felicia Felix-Mentor, who had apparently returned from the dead after having been buried for thirty years. Hurston, like other ethnographers after her, was open to the possibility that zombification was a clinical fact, brought on by the administration of powerful psychotropic drugs unknown to Western medicine.

Whether or not that is the case, it is clear that the zombie as a symbol in voodoo arises directly out of, and comments upon, the experience of slavery: the zombie is a mindless worker, completely in thrall to a malign master. While zombies may be everywhere now, they were uncommon monsters in early and mid-twentieth-century horror cinema—but when they appeared, it was always in the context of slavery. The first zombie film was Victor Halperin's *White Zombie* (1932), set on Haiti and starring the great Béla Lugosi as Murder Legendre, a white slaver who commands an army of zombies to work his sugar plantation. Jacques Tourneur's *I Walked With a Zombie* (1943), one of a series of atmospheric horrors produced by Val Lewton for RKO Pictures, is a Caribbean rewriting of *Jane Eyre* in which meek Canadian nurse Frances Dee finds herself working on the island of San Sebastian, enmeshed in a world of voodoo and zombies (the African American actor Darby Jones gives a chillingly memorable performance as the zombie Carrefour), to the accompaniment of an ongoing musical commentary by calypso singer Sir Lancelot. As an example of what we would call today a postcolonial rescripting of *Jane Eyre*, *I Walked With a Zombie* predates Jean Rhys's *Wide Sargasso Sea* by over twenty years, and must surely have influenced Rhys in writing her pioneering novel. In 1966 (interestingly, the same year as the publication of *Wide Sargasso Sea*), Hammer Studios released *The Plague of the Zombies*, directed by John Gilling, in which Cornish squire John Carson returns from

Haiti as a voodoo adept, and sets about creating a zombie workforce as cheap labour for his tin-mine.

Wes Craven's 1988 *The Serpent and the Rainbow* is set on Haiti. The film is loosely based on Wade Davis's ethnographic study of the same title, and comments directly on the barbarities of the dictatorial Duvalier regime, which ruled Haiti from 1957 to 1986, and which was reputed to have cemented its power through its secret police, the *Tonton Macoute*'s use of voodoo and zombification. But *The Serpent and the Rainbow* is quite self-consciously an anomaly, an historical outlier. Within a couple of years of the release of *The Plague of the Zombies*, the political meaning of zombie culture was about to change dramatically, and forever.

In 1968, George A. Romero, an independent film-maker from Pittsburgh of great political intelligence, released *Night of the Living Dead*, and the modern horror film was born. The film opens with a bickering brother and sister, Johnny and Barbara, driving to a rural Pennsylvania cemetery to visit their father's grave. At the graveside, they see what appears to be an old man shuffling towards them, and Johnny, doing an excellent Boris Karloff impersonation, utters the film's most celebrated line: '*They're coming to get you, Barbara!*' And they are. The old man is in fact a zombie freshly risen from his grave, who attacks and kills Johnny. Barbara manages to escape to a nearby farmhouse, but spends the rest of the film catatonic. In the farmhouse, a cast of characters led by Ben (Duane Jones), a heroic African American, repulses the onslaught of what seems to be a never-ending wave of the undead, who have (in the film's most startling departure from traditional zombie lore) turned cannibalistic. But the real danger, it seems, lurks within the farmhouse itself, as the surviving characters argue and fight among themselves for leadership, and over whether they should fortify the farmhouse and stand and fight, or hide in the cellar. Over the course of a long night, the zombies attempt again and again to break into the farmhouse, turning the film into what has been described as 'a symphony of psychotic hands'—the hands (two of them belonging to the Returned Johnny) that reach out, trying to break through doors and boarded-up windows, tearing at human flesh. (It's the nearest cinema has ever come to rendering a genuine nightmare in its relentless sense of impending doom.) As dawn breaks, a posse arrives led by a redneck sheriff. They shoot the zombies in the head (that's how you stop them—another pioneering invention from Romero), and burn the corpses on a gigantic funeral pyre. Ben, stumbling from the farmhouse having survived the Night of the Living Dead, is shot in the head by one of the posse. In the film's closing shot, we see his corpse being hoisted on to the pyre with a meathook.

There is much to say about *Night of the Living Dead*, which might be the most influential horror film ever made. It effectively introduced in their modern forms the two qualities which define much subsequent horror—nihilism and gore. *Night* was made on a tiny budget of $114,000, and one of Romero's backers was a Pittsburgh butcher, whose contribution to the film is there onscreen for all to see, as the zombies munch away on entrails and various pieces of offal (by the third instalment of Romero's *Living Dead* series,

1985's *Day of the Dead*, there was reputedly so much rotting offal on the set that the cast were vomiting between takes). It is also a film with a radical political critique of contemporary American society, mired in an increasingly unpopular and unwinnable war in Vietnam, and struggling domestically to assimilate the implications of the civil rights movement. The year 1968 was an American *annus horribilis*, with the assassinations of Martin Luther King and Robert Kennedy following on from those of JFK and Malcolm X a few years previously, and in *Night of the Living Dead* America seemed to have got the film it deserved, a film better-placed than any other to reflect its horror, its justified disillusionment with authority, its racism (it's a film which ends with a heroic black leader shot by racist white authority figures). It became a major success on the American drive-in circuit, with young audiences flocking to see a film which so closely represented their own sensibilities.

In the image of the walking dead returned to devour the living, Romero clearly felt he had hit upon *the* great all-purpose metaphor for representing contemporary America, and so has continued to remake the film ever since: *Dawn of the Dead* (1978), *Day of the Dead* (1985), *Land of the Dead* (2005), *Diary of the Dead* (2007), *Survival of the Dead* (2009). All are worth watching, but *Dawn* is Romero's masterpiece, and probably the single film most responsible for creating today's zombie culture. For one thing, by 1978 Romero had started working with make-up genius Tom Savini, the man who really brought gore and splatter to horror cinema in all its eyeball-gouging, head-severing, entrail-spilling glory (Savini had served in the US army in Vietnam as a combat photographer, an experience which he admits definitively shaped his cinematic career). But more than this, *Dawn* offers perhaps the most powerful, devastating, and influential critique of consumer culture in any work of modern art. Here, the Night of the Living Dead has turned into an all-out Zombie Apocalypse, as the dead have overrun America. A small group of survivors takes shelter in a gigantic shopping mall, where they spend their time alternately browsing the aisles and stocking up on consumer goods, and fighting off the zombie hordes who also want to get into the mall as it's the place they feel most at home.

Dawn is probably best viewed as a combination of a delirious Swiftian satire and a Frankfurt School treatise: this is Theodor Adorno's Culture Industry, once again red in tooth and claw. *Dawn* has, in fact, provided cultural commentators with one of the most effective discourses for critiquing consumer culture. It's no accident that, when Curtis White wrote his own brilliant, Adorno-inflected critique of the modern American Culture Industry, *The Middle Mind* (2004), it should be subtitled *Why Consumer Culture is Turning Us Into the Living Dead*. Scarcely less brilliant was Charlie Brooker's rebarbative attack on media culture, *Dead Set* (2008), in which zombies attack the studio where reality TV nightmare *Big Brother* is being filmed. (The previous year, Brooker had published a volume of essays entitled *Dawn of the Dumb*.)

Dead Set is one example of what has become a proliferation of zombie culture since the millennium. In 2003, the writer Max Brooks published *The Zombie Survival Guide*, a practical handbook to coping with the forthcoming zombie apocalypse. This captured the public imagination, and was the precursor of Brooks's bestselling novel *World War Z: An Oral History of the Zombie War* (2006), which used the kinds of documentary narrative techniques horror has deployed since the publication of *Frankenstein, Jekyll and Hyde*, and (especially) *Dracula* in the nineteenth century, but which to a contemporary readership may seem like the novelistic equivalent of horror cinema's dominant post-millennial 'found footage' technique (see Chapter 6). The zombie apocalypse is at the centre of the brilliantly successful TV series *The Walking Dead* (first broadcast 2010), and provides the overarching narrative threat for the even more successful *Game of Thrones* (first broadcast 2011). Numerous films of the 2010s have focused on the outbreak or aftermath of a zombie pandemic, from the troubled film adaptation of *World War Z* (2013) to the surprisingly affecting Arnold Schwarzenegger vehicle *Maggie* (2015) to the remarkable *The Girl With All the Gifts* (2016). Advertisements, apparently straight-faced (it is impossible to tell with certainty), have begun to appear online for 'Zombie-Proof' houses.

Contemporary zombie culture has, as I suggested, gained especial resonance since the global financial crisis of 2007, as an expression of personal disempowerment and apocalyptic terror. To borrow a phrase which is usually attributed to the philosopher Slavoj Žižek, but which has been deployed by commentators both on zombies and on the contemporary cultural politics: it is easier to imagine the end of the world than the end of capitalism. And so it is that, following Romero's *Dawn of the Dead*, zombification has become one of our major metaphors for thinking through the contemporary scene and our own individual helplessness in the face of vast economic forces which we may feel are inimical to the good life, or of the seemingly inevitable ecological catastrophes brought on by those forces. The zombie apocalypse, it seems, really is upon us.

2

The Occult and
the Supernatural

We live, according to the famous pronouncement of the sociologist Max Weber, in a *disenchanted* world—that is, a world without the possibility of magic. In 1917 Weber wrote that 'the fate of our times is characterized by rationalism and intellectualization and, above all, by the "disenchantment of the world"'. Writing as he was in the middle of the first distinctively modern 'total war', it is easy to see how Weber was responding to the carnage of the machine age: 'we need no longer rely on magic as a device for mastering spirits or pleading with them', he wrote elsewhere, since 'Calculation and technical equipment do the job.' Since the Enlightenment, Weber believed, the dominant philosophical narrative for understanding the nature of reality was rational materialism, or (as it is sometimes termed) scientific naturalism. For the materialist, anything else was simply hocus-pocus, discredited nonsense.

In the same year, 1917, Arthur Conan Doyle also responded to the Great War by writing the first of a series of books on a subject which was to dominate the last years of his life: spiritualism. The connections between spiritualism and the war were, for Doyle, vividly real. The war, he believed, had been brought about by 'the organized materialism of Germany', since 'when religion is dead, materialism becomes active, and what active materialism may produce has been seen in Germany'. Spiritualism, for Doyle, was '[by] far the greatest development of human experience which the world has ever seen . . . by far the greatest event since the death of Christ . . . an enormous new development, the greatest in the history of mankind'. Here, for many, was a revealed truth which, through the achievements of psychics and mediums, had convincingly demonstrated the survival of the human personality after death, and the existence of an 'Other World'. This was the world of spirits, coexisting with our own, separated from our own material world merely by the veil of perception, the limitations of our own senses.

To understand these responses, we need to go back fifty years or so earlier. The publication in 1859 of Charles Darwin's *The Origin of Species* caused an intellectual, emotional, and psychological shock to Victorian society, whose resonances are still felt today. In its immediate aftermath, Darwinism, and the climate of rationalist secular materialism of which it was understood as the pinnacle, brought about a crisis of faith. The bleak implications of scientific naturalism—that humanity was merely an ape adapted with unusual (but inevitably temporary) success to its particular niche; that there was no soul, no afterlife, perhaps no God, and therefore no greater purpose or meaning to existence—were understandably psychologically unbearable for many of the people who came into contact with them.

One response or reaction to this was a re-emphasis in the second half of the nineteenth century on hidden meanings, concealed or rejected knowledge, and other worlds. The 'new revelation' of spiritualism, Doyle maintained, was 'absolutely fatal . . . to materialism'. It is in ideas such as these that we see the beginnings of a powerful modern counter-Enlightenment tendency, which the theologian Christopher Partridge, drawing on Weber, has termed *The Re-Enchantment of the West*.

It is no accident, then, that these Victorian decades were also witness to the great modern flowering of the distinct but overlapping practices of spiritualism, occultism, and supernaturalism. The formations of the Society for Psychical Research (1881), the Hermetic Order of the Golden Dawn (1888), and the Folklore Society (1878) all date from this period—the last-named codifying a renewed interest in folklore studies (often with a distinctively nationalist approach) from scholars, poets, and anthologists such as Andrew Lang, Fiona Macleod, Sir William and Lady Jane Wilde, Joseph Jacobs, or W. B. Yeats. It is also the period which saw the development of the modern ghost story, from Charles Dickens and Sheridan Le Fanu to M. R. James (whose first story, 'Canon Alberic's Scrap-Book', appeared in 1895), and of the supernatural tale ('Carmilla', 1871; *The Great God Pan*, 1894; *Dracula*, 1897). The scene was set by the publication in 1848 of Catherine Crowe's bestselling compendium *The Night Side of Nature*, whose contents offer a representative sampling of the supernatural, including haunted houses, precognition, doppelgängers, and poltergeists.

What is the meaning of magic? For the great Victorian anthropologist and hard-line scientific materialist J. G. Frazer, it was a product of the pre-civilized mind. Primitive societies, he asserts, are characterized by their inability to distinguish magic from science:

> The principles of association are excellent in themselves, and indeed absolutely essential to the workings of the human mind. Legitimately applied they yield science; illegitimately applied they yield magic, the bastard sister of science. It is therefore a truism, almost a tautology, to say that all magic is necessarily false and barren; for if it were ever to become true, it would no longer be magic but science.

But not everybody saw it that way. Magic, wrote the Victorian magus Éliphas Lévi, far from being 'the jugglery of mounte-banks' or 'the hallucinations of disordered minds', is a rigor-ous scientific doctrine, 'the exact and absolute science of Nature and her laws...the science of the ancient magi'. Is magic outmoded thinking, or even childish nonsense, or is it a means of apprehending concealed or neglected realities? For the distinguished historian of magic Lynn Thorndike, 'it represented a way of looking at the world'. Magic is ante-cedent to theology—it is older than the gods. Civilization itself, Thorndike believes, has its origins in magic. Many of our religions, our arts, our sciences, as well as our medicine, mathematics, and law, have their deep origins in magic. Sorcerers were the first professional class.

Of all modern cultural forms, horror is perhaps the most open to the possibilities of magic and the supernatural. Horror tells us that there are more things in heaven and earth than are dreamt of in our philosophy—at least, if our philosophy is a materialist one—and that the world contains (or in extreme form, that our lives are governed by) certain inexplicable forces or unaccountable spirits which we can attempt to appease or even control, but which cannot be encompassed within any rational or scientific model of reality. While a major work such as Henry James's haunted house classic *The Turn of the Screw* draws much of its uncanny power from its undecidability and ambiguity, the tension in which it holds two competing interpretations (supernatural and psychological) of the events it narrates, this is relatively unusual. Generally, though some of its characters may be sceptics, the genre itself is a true believer.

One of horror's classic plots involves the re-education of a rational materialist sceptic, often some form of academic or 'expert'—indeed, part of horror's appeal for some lies in its repudiation of traditional, hierarchical, or institutional forms of knowledge. In M. R. James's 'Oh, Whistle, and I'll Come to You, My Lad', for example, Parkins, the rational materialist Professor of Ontography (that is, 'Professor of Reality'), is taught a comprehensive lesson in metaphysics after unearthing an ancient whistle concealed beneath the altar of a ruined Templar preceptory. At high table in his Oxbridge college, Parkins is dismissive of the supernatural: 'I freely own that I do *not* like careless talk about what you call ghosts. A man in my position . . . cannot be too careful about appearing to sanction the current beliefs on such subjects. . . . I hold that any semblance, any appearance of concession to the view that such things might exist is equivalent to a renunciation of all that I hold most sacred.'

At the close of the story, after his encounter with the bed sheet ghost summoned by the ancient whistle he uncovers, 'the Professor's views on certain points are less clear cut than they used to be.'

In this chapter, then, we will look at a few instances of horror's serious engagement with the occult, magic, and the supernatural, and of the ideas, beliefs, images, and anxieties that this conjures with or summons up. As a mark of respect, it is only proper that we begin at the top, with the Devil himself.

The Devil

As I suggested in Chapter 1, Stephen King's novels of the 1970s enact the clash of the traditional 'Old European' sensibilities of Gothic and horror with the pop-cultural sens-ibilities of American modernity. In *'Salem's Lot* (1975), this is in part articulated through the representative figure of a Catholic priest, Father Callahan, who is troubled by the contemporary sociological orientation of his vocation in the wake of the modernizing theology ushered in by the Second Vatican Council (1962–5): 'he was being forced into the conclusion that there was no EVIL in the world at all but only evil—or perhaps (evil)'. The novel forces Father Callahan into a confrontation with old-school, pre-Vatican II, European EVIL in the person of the vampire Barlow—a confrontation which he loses decisively, as, no longer undergirded by faith, sanctity, or metaphysics, the trappings of his vocation are empty symbols in his hands. Father Callahan closes the novel wandering the earth cursed, the

Mark of Cain placed upon his forehead by Barlow, unable to cross the threshold of a church.

What is the nature and the function of evil in a world supposedly governed by divine grace? These are the questions posed by theodicy, that branch of theology which sets out, in the words of John Milton, to 'justify the ways of God to men'. Is evil merely the absence of good (a lack, a negative, a non-being), or is it a positive, moral force at large in creation? These are issues which have long troubled theologians and religious commentators. In a polytheistic order (a pantheon of many gods), or even in a dualistic religion (one which posits the coexistence of forces of good and evil, light and darkness—such as Zoroastrianism or Jedi), the nature of evil is worrying but readily comprehensible—it is one of a number of forces (two or more) holding sway over creation. But in a monistic religion such as Christianity, which posits one all-powerful creator God, evil is a real categorical problem. If evil exists, then it can only have been created by God, as there can be nothing outside of God's creation. If so, for what purpose? Can a God of absolute goodness and benevolence have created evil? Conversely, to posit that evil does not exist (it is an absence of goodness, no more) seems intellectually and emotionally unsatisfying in the face of the lived reality of cruelty and atrocity.

As Satan's biographer Peter Stanford suggests, the Devil is 'a popular figure, not a dogmatic abstraction, and has come alive not in learned tomes or seminary debates, but in the lives of the faithful, terrifying, omnipresent and grotesque, evil incarnate'. In large part this is because the questions posed by theodicy are so difficult and painful as to prove essentially unanswerable, or answerable only by what can often seem slippery evasions, or through arguments and assertions which are simply inadequate to the task. As the theologian Charles T. Mathewes has observed, in the face of atrocities, 'to say that "God is love" can seem like handing daisies to a psychopath'. Thus, mainstream, official, or institutionalized theology tends to avoid these questions. It has, in other words, ceded the territory of evil to popular culture: this is the domain of the Devil.

The historian of Satanism Ruben van Luijk notes that 'Only toward the end of the nineteenth century did the word "Satanism" come to hold the significance that it still has, for historians of religion, B-film directors, and the general public alike, namely, the intentional and explicit worship of Satan.' This is entirely in keeping with the modern resurgence in the occult and supernatural which we discussed at the beginning of the chapter. But the development of a body of ritual and practice associated with Satanism, and with the occult more generally, has its origins in antiquity. Demons—personifications of specific aspects of evil—seem to have developed out of the attributes of some of the gods as classical thought moved from polytheism towards the direction of dualism. The underworld had traditionally carried associations of fertility because of its connection with the cycle of the seasons, death and rebirth, and thus the location of the Devil and demons in a subterranean hell linked them with sexuality. Many of the rites associated with pagan deities—with Dionysus, Cybele, or Mithras—contained elements which were to become standard in the alleged practices of witches and heretics.

Accounts of the worship of Satan tend to have a lurid and sensationalist element which betray their origins at the schlockier end of popular culture. These can take the form of bogus or embellished exposés of Satanic practices, from *The Devil in the XIXth Century* by 'Dr Bataille', which shocked Paris in the 1890s, to Rollo Ahmed's *The Black Art* (1936), a major influence on the thinking of the great mid-century novelist of pulp Satanism, Dennis Wheatley. Accounts of Black Masses tend to suggest inversions of the Roman Catholic mass, as in this description by Rollo Ahmed:

> At eleven o'clock precisely the officiating priest began the Mass backwards, ending at the stroke of midnight. The Host used on these occasions was black and three-pointed. No wine was consecrated, but the priest drank filthy water or, according to some accounts, water in which the body of an unbaptised child had been thrown. He used no crucifix, but formed the sign of the cross on the ground with his left foot.

Part of the undeniable appeal of modern Satanic popular culture is the opportunity it affords for representations of transgressive and taboo sexuality. In Matthew Lewis's enduringly popular Gothic shocker *The Monk* (1796), the Devil tempts the virtuous holy man Ambrosio into orgies of eroticized Mariolatry, rape, incest, and thinly veiled necrophilia. In Rollo Ahmed's Black Mass, 'The ordinary participants, inflamed with drugs and drink, maddened with blood and sadistic excitement, would certainly have had no thought but of expressing their lowest and filthiest impulses, and of wallowing in a mad phantasmagoria of sexual lust.' As

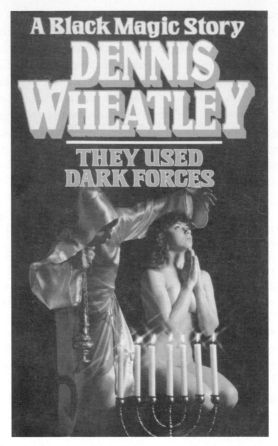

Figure 4. A characteristically lurid Dennis Wheatley paperback.

their covers make all too clear, a large part of the appeal of Wheatley's bestselling series of Satanic thrillers, which sold around fifty million copies in the middle decades of the twentieth century, was their sexual exploitativeness (Figure 4).

In a manner which will be familiar from the Introduction, part of the transgressive power of these accounts of forbidden Satanic rites lies not only in their violation of taboos, but also in their representation of abjection. In a conscious inversion of deeply held concepts of pollution, unclean bodily matter is put to ritual use. One modern account of these practices notes that 'the rituals...involve blood, urine, feces and semen'. At their most extreme, they contain accounts of ritual human sacrifice and cannibalism, sometimes involving children:

> Most of the sacrificial victims of the Black Mass were women [Ahmed asserts], but young children and even babies were not exempt, and occasionally men were butchered as well. All were slain with ingenious torture and cruelty, their bowels and entrails being literally torn out, while, when women were the victims, the reproductive organs were chosen as the point of torture. Little children were treated in the same way; the Devil, or at least his followers, evidently taking unholy pleasure in the sacrifice of the young.

Given the extreme nature of the images and ideas it produces, it is perhaps not surprising that horror, as we have seen, is often accompanied by moral panics and censorship. Sensational popular culture, whether produced by self-proclaimed 'experts' such as Ahmed, or by popular writers and filmmakers, can find itself implicated in, and informing, social and political discourse. In what is perhaps the first modern example of the recurring horror-induced moral panic, *The Monk* was accused of blasphemy, an allegation sufficiently serious for Lewis himself to oversee the publication of a new, bowdlerized edition of his novel in 1798. Writing in the 1930s, Rollo Ahmed was at pains to stress that black magic is an ongoing practice in modern society, and that Satanists remain all around us, often in positions of influence. The 'Pizzagate' affair of 2016, alleging a widespread conspiracy of paedophilic Satanic Ritual Abuse, with the participation of high-ranking American political and establishment figures, was not the first and will certainly not be the last moral panic of its kind, and culminated in shots being fired at the Comet Ping Pong pizza restaurant in Washington, DC. However absurd their details may sometimes seem, these scandals can have real human consequences, be it children removed from their parents by social services, or in the case of Pizzagate a shooting which could easily have ended tragically.

A belief in the existence of the Devil bestows an existential certainty and meaning. Stephen King's Father Callahan is one of a number of Catholic priests appearing in works of post-Vatican II horror, from *The Exorcist* to *The Amityville Horror*, often religious modernists trained in the secular disciplines of psychology, sociology, or anthropology who find themselves completely unequipped to deal with positive, personified EVIL, and are all destroyed by their encounters with Satanic forces. In a way which might be strangely reassuring for many of its audience, horror offers no ambiguity in the face of evil. The word 'devil' comes from the Greek *diabolos*, 'adversary' (or 'slanderer'), which is itself a rendering of the Hebrew *satan*, 'opponent' (originally, a descriptor rather than a proper noun: one's opponent was 'a *satan*', not '*the* Devil'). Satan, Belial, Azazel, Samyaza, Beelzebub, Lucifer, Asmodeus, Mephistopheles, Keyser Söze. The Devil has many names, and has taken many forms, but he is real, an active agent at large in the world, and he wants your soul.

To 'the Jesuits, for teaching me to think'. So reads the close of William Peter Blatty's acknowledgements to *The Exorcist* (1971). A series of epigraphs, beginning with Luke's account of the Gadarene swine, through a transcript of an FBI wiretap of a conversation about brutal Mafia torture and murder, to an account of atrocities committed against Catholic priests in Maoist China, and closing with the words 'Dachau Auschwitz Buchenwald', makes clear by juxtaposition the novel's belief in the direct relationship between demonic possession and modern evil. The novel understands modern atrocities and brutalities as a direct manifestation of the Devil, an active force for 'radical evil' at large in the world, not a sociological abstraction or a theological sophistry to signify the mere absence of God.

William Friedkin's 1973 adaptation of the novel is rightly understood as one of the most powerful horror films ever made. Its indelible images of radical Satanic evil literally inscribing itself on the flesh of the adolescent Regan MacNeil in scars and mutilation, disfigurements, and even words understandably proved too much for many audiences, some of whom believed that watching the film was itself an encounter with Satanic forces. The evangelist Billy Graham believed that the very film itself was possessed by the Devil. And yet *The Exorcist* was made with the support and participation of the Catholic Church, and features among its cast a number of Jesuit priests playing versions of themselves. The success of the film contributed directly to a spike in applications for the Catholic priesthood in the 1970s, and for obvious reasons. In both book and film, the priest-psychiatrist Father Karras and his medical colleagues exhaust every somatic and psychological explanation for Regan's condition before confronting the obvious fact that the Devil is real, and it is only through the traditional rites and sacraments of Catholicism that he can be defeated.

The Exorcist was an important part of a post-war cultural phenomenon. The artistic and commercial success of Roman Polanski's *Rosemary's Baby* in 1968, based on Ira Levin's best-selling novel of the previous year, is often credited as marking the beginning of the 1970s' 'satanic screen'—and, along with Romero's genuinely radical *Night of the Living Dead* (also 1968), is seen by many as the foundational work of modern horror cinema. *Rosemary's Baby* has nothing like the degree of religious horror to be found in *The Exorcist*. Levin's novel in particular does gesture towards the travails of Catholicism in 1960s America, but in not very much detail. Rosemary Woodhouse is 'Catholic but no longer observing'; her family had 'not forgiven her for (*a*) marrying a Protestant, (*b*) marrying in a civil ceremony, and (*c*) having a mother-in-law who had had two divorces and was now married to a Jew up in Canada.' She has nightmares about her convent education, and one startling dream sequence in which the Pope, the Devil, and JFK seem all to be conflated.

In 1977, Jeffrey Burton Russell, one of the Devil's greatest historians, wrote scornfully about *The Exorcist* for presenting 'a Devil who is stupid enough to choose to possess a little girl rather than a national government, which would enable him to do much greater harm to the world'. This seems like a reasonable observation—albeit that it rather misses the point of *The Exorcist*—and is certainly representative of the position of much modern popular cultural theodicy, which is, as we have seen, keen to explore the possibility of large-scale political Satanic conspiracies. *Rosemary's Baby* is an important cinematic example of the major preoccupation in modern horror with the birth and upbringing of the Antichrist. In this specific concern, *Rosemary's Baby* anticipates works coming out of a Protestant or even an Evangelical tradition, such as *The Omen* (1976), and in our own century Tim LaHaye and Jerry B. Jenkins's monster-selling series of Evangelical eschatological thrillers, *Left Behind* (1995–2007), in which the Antichrist is a Romanian politician who gets elected Secretary General of the United Nations.

The Omen, in particular, is a film which propounds, through the influence of the Evangelical pastors Robert Munger and Don Williams, who are both listed in the credits as 'religious adviser [*sic*] to the producers', a covert ideological agenda that is very much in tune with the apocalypticism of the religious right. *The Omen* is also markedly anti-Catholic. When Cathy Thorn (Lee Remick), wife of the American ambassador to Rome, loses her baby in childbirth, a Catholic priest suggests to her husband Robert (Gregory Peck) that they secretly switch the dead child with another born at the same time, whose mother has died. What Thorn has not been told, however, is that the baby who is to become young Damien Thorn was born of a jackal. Father Brennan (played by Patrick Troughton), the crazed Catholic priest who was present at the birth, has a birthmark on his thigh which reads 666. The implication of the film is obvious: that the Vatican, which not only nurtures and protects the Antichrist, but places him where he is in a position to do the greatest harm, as the son of 'the future President of the United States', is in league with the Devil. The film closes at Robert Thorn's funeral, with little Damien holding the hands of the President and First Lady.

Ghosts and Spirits

Satanism is of necessity a limit case, an extreme far shore of belief. Being a believer in—or even a practitioner of—the supernatural or the occult does not necessarily, of course, make you a Satanist. Nor, for that matter, does enjoying books about magic, although there have been calls in the UK to ban the Harry Potter books from classrooms because, according to Tom Bennett, an advisor to the British government on matters of educational behaviour, the series 'normalises acts of magic' and even 'glorifies witchcraft' for some of its readers: 'There are many parents who are uncomfortable with their children discussing or looking at or reading anything at all to do with the occult.' In the US, fringe members of the religious right have conducted several public burnings of the Harry Potter books. And yet, as I suggested at the beginning of the chapter, most religions—and in fact even the very concept of religion—have their deep origins in magical belief and ritual. For many, perhaps most, people of faith, a belief in the reality of the supernatural is by no means incompatible with, say, deeply held Christianity. As any reader of the Gospels—and most particularly of St Mark, generally held to be the oldest of the Gospels and thus the closest in time to the events it describes—will testify, exorcism, the casting out of demons, was a major component of Christ's earthly mission. While there are certainly those who remain willing to ascribe a variety of physical and psychological illnesses to demonic possession, for most of us an actual encounter with the supernatural is likely to mean ghosts and spirits, not devils and demons.

'Do you believe in ghosts?' 'Have you ever seen a ghost?' As someone with a research interest in the supernatural, I get asked these questions all the time (my simplistic answers are 'no' and 'no', but I have, and prefer, more nuanced ones). According to a 2016 YouGov survey, more British people believe in ghosts than in 'a Creator' (interestingly, only 40 per cent of self-identified British Christians claim to believe in a Creator, according to the same survey). According to a 2013 Harris Poll, 42 per cent of Americans believe in ghosts, while the figure for Britons is 52 per cent.

If anything, I am surprised that these figures are so low, as a belief in ghosts is a consistent component of human culture. *The Epic of Gilgamesh*, the Mesopotamian text which is perhaps the oldest surviving work of literature, dating from 1500–2000 BC, closes with the warrior-king Gilgamesh meeting the spirit of his dead companion Enkidu, who gives him an account of the underworld. In the Old Testament Book of I Samuel, composed around 800 BC but describing events from the eleventh century BC, King Saul seeks advice on the eve of a battle with the Philistines from the Witch of Endor. The Witch summons up the ghost of Samuel, who asks Saul, 'Why hast thou disquieted me, to bring me up?' In Homer's *Odyssey* (eighth century BC), Odysseus, journeying through the underworld, encounters the shade of his mother Anticlea, who tells him:

> You are only witnessing here the law of our mortal nature, when we come to die. We no longer have sinews keeping the bones and flesh together, but once the life-force is departed from our white bones, all is consumed by the fierce heat of the blazing fire, and the soul slips away like a dream and flutters on the air.

In the *Eumenides*, the final part of the *Oresteia* trilogy of Aeschylus (fifth–sixth century BC), the first of the great Greek tragedians, the ghost of Clytemnestra awakens the Furies to act as instruments of her vengeance on her matricidal son Orestes. There seems to be no established body of religion, mythology, or folklore that does not allow for the existence of ghosts. Ghosts, like horror more generally, are intrinsic to civilization.

For a modern audience, at least, there should in principle be something comforting about the appearance of ghosts, an assurance that there is a world beyond the material, that death is not the end. After all, as Homer's Anticlea avows, a ghost is the soul slipping away from its bodily moorings, fluttering on the air. In his book *The Concept of Mind* (1949), the philosopher Gilbert Ryle coined the phrase 'the ghost in the machine' as a description of a dualistic view of (material) body and (non-material) mind. Ryle intended the term to be part of a critique of the fallacy of mind/body dualism, but it has entered popular discourse as a resonant metaphor, encapsulating the sense many have that the workings of consciousness are something categorically quite separate from the corporeal matter of our flesh. In 1981, the rock band The Police, whose lead singer, Sting, was rather given to displays of his erudition, released an album entitled *Ghost in the Machine*; its opening track was 'Spirits in the Material World'. For many, the concept of the ghost in the machine—what spiritualists would have called the survival of the human personality after death—is a reassuring one.

There can, in fact, be something comforting about certain ghosts and ghost stories. Telling ghost stories can have an apotropaic function—that is, it serves to ward off evil. Their very generic status gives ghost stories an air of participatory ritual. Ghost stories are told on the longest nights, when the forces of darkness are at their most powerful. This is why there is such a strong connection between ghost stories and Christmas. 'A Christmas Carol' is simultaneously the most celebrated ghost story and the most celebrated Christmas story, and its publication in 1843 inaugurated a popular series of Dickensian Christmas tales, most of which were supernatural. Many of M. R. James's ghost stories were first told on Christmas Eve, around the fire to a select group of colleagues and students in King's College Cambridge. In 'Oh, Whistle', Professor Parkins unearths the titular supernatural artefact on 'the feast day of St. Thomas the Apostle'—that is, 21 December, the winter solstice. Since the 1970s, viewers of BBC television have regularly enjoyed a series of 'Ghost Stories for Christmas', many of them adaptations of the works of M. R. James.

Although belonging to a non-material order, ghosts can also have a material dimension, or leave physical traces, often of the category-violating disgusting kind we encountered in the Introduction—from the viscid 'ectoplasm' detected by spiritualists and psychical researchers to the slime of *Ghostbusters*.

Ghosts are spiritual; ghosts can be unpleasantly material; but mostly, of course, ghosts are terrifying. In part, this is because they carry with them a sense of desolation, or of disjuncture. In M. R. James's story 'Lost Hearts' there is an utterly despairing image of a ghost boy, 'a thin shape, with black hair and ragged clothing, [who] raised his arms in the air with an appearance of menace and of unappeasable hunger and longing'. As James writes elsewhere, 'a withered heart makes an ugly thin ghost'. Ghosts are severed from the bonds of human kindness, family, and love. It is the hollowness, the existential emptiness of the ghostly that disturbs. This is what Jacob Marley's ghost tells Scrooge:

> It is required of every man . . . that the spirit within him should walk abroad among his fellow men, and travel far and wide; and if that spirit goes not forth in life, it is condemned to do so after death. It is doomed to wander through the world—oh, woe is me!—and witness what it cannot share, but might have shared on earth, and turned to happiness!

Ghosts are *condemned* to walk the earth because they are excluded from the divine, barred entrance to heaven. This is the case with Hamlet's Father:

> I am thy father's spirit,
> Doom'd for a certain time to walk the night,
> And for the day confin'd to fast in fires,

> Till the foul crimes done in my days of nature
> Are burnt and purged away.

Traditionally, then, the appearance of ghosts served a narrative or moral purpose. Like Clytemnestra's ghost or the ghost of Hamlet's Father, they appeared in order to right wrongs, atone for crimes, or correct injustices. These ghosts can be violent, vengeful, fearsome, unappeasable. Like Banquo's ghost in *Macbeth*, they could appear as a warning or an omen, often portending death. Or, like the ghosts of Samuel or Anticlea, they came back from the dead bearing privileged information, including prophecies of future events. Some ghosts, like that of Jacob Marley, do all three at once.

But not all ghosts are purposeful narrative actors, and this is especially true of some of their modern manifestations, who are often characterized by the very arbitrariness of their hauntings. For the reasons discussed at the beginning of the chapter, the second half of the nineteenth century saw a renewed interest in ghosts. The historian Owen Davies has argued that this Victorian ghost may represent a new development in thinking about the supernatural in its very *purposelessness*. In his 1894 study of psychical research, the folklorist Andrew Lang concluded that the modern ghost was 'a purposeless creature', appearing 'nobody knows why; he has no message to deliver, no secret crime to reveal, no appointment to keep, no treasure to disclose, no commissions to be executed, and, as an almost invariable rule, he does not speak, even if you speak to him'.

The teenagers in Hideo Nakata's *Ring* cannot in any meaningful way be said to deserve the terrifying supernatural visitation of the cursed videocassette, unless we count sheer curiosity as a moral failing (which M. R. James, the greatest of all ghost story writers, perhaps did—one of his most celebrated stories, and the volume which contains it, is called *A Warning to the Curious*). Similarly, unless we take a very stern view of low-level obnoxiousness, the protagonists of many modern ghost stories, from Nigel Kneale's *The Stone Tape* (1972) to *The Blair Witch Project* (1999) to *Insidious* (2010), are arbitrary victims, all stumbling as if by accident into the haunted locations which prove their undoing.

Buried in certain spaces and objects, it seems, waiting to be uncovered, as though by an archaeological excavation, the past and its spirits lurk. The appearance of a ghost is the eruption of the past into the present, and troubles our sense of progress, of a one-directional arrow of time. Marley's ghost promises Scrooge on Christmas Eve that he will be visited by three ghosts on three nights: 'Expect the first tomorrow when the bell tolls One....Expect the second on the next night at the same hour. The third upon the next night when the last stroke of twelve has ceased to vibrate.' And yet, in the time-less spirit world, these three separate nights all happen simultaneously, and when Scrooge awakens from his last visitation, it is Christmas morning. In the spirit world the arrow of time can fly in all directions, and so precognition, the uncanny possibility of being haunted by the future, is an important component of the ghost story, as when Scrooge is haunted by the Ghost of Christmas Yet to Come, or when the protagonist of another Dickens story, 'The Signal-Man', is haunted by recurring visions of his own death. Ghosts are time out of joint.

3

Horror and the Body

What is the locus of fear? *Where* is fear? In Chapter 2 we looked at some forms of supernatural horror. In these works, the threat is radically Other, emanating from the outside, from different categories of being or philosophies of existence. But running alongside this is a tradition of internal horror, in which that which we have to fear is inside us. Sometimes, this internal fear emerges out of the labyrinthine ways of our own minds, showing the uncanny means by which we can be alien to ourselves. This will be the subject of Chapter 4. But sometimes, as we have seen, it is our own bodies that are horrifying to us. Bodies, I have suggested, can be viewed as symbolic systems, sites of meaning, power, threat, and anxiety. Viewed in this way, our skin functions as a boundary, as we have seen—a vulnerable, malleable, porous, leaky border between inside and outside, self and other, a site of abjection and of pain. In this chapter, we will look more closely at the horror of the body.

Metamorphosis

To begin thinking about horror and the body, we will look at those narratives in which the body changes form, from the 'normal' to the 'monstrous' body. Often, these narratives record the transformation from the civilized, social human body to the violent, uncontrollable beast body. The werewolf is the *locus classicus* of this kind of narrative.

The word *lycanthrope* derives from the myth of Lycaon, king of Arcadia in the Peloponnesian Peninsula of Greece. The best-known version of the tale is to be found in Ovid's *Metamorphoses*. Lycaon, 'well known for savagery', is cursed by Zeus after attempting to feed human flesh to the king of the gods:

> The king himself flies in terror, and gaining the silent fields, howls aloud, attempting in vain to speak. His mouth of itself gathers foam, and with his accustomed greed for blood he turns against the sheep, delighting still in slaughter. His garments change to shaggy hair, his arms to legs. He turns to a wolf, and yet retains some of his former shape. There is the same grey hair, the same fierce face, the same gleaming eyes, the same picture of beastly savagery.

There are several different extant versions of the Lycaon myth, often serving to heighten his depravity. According to the Greek geographer Pausanias, 'Lycaon brought a human baby to the altar of Lycean Zeus, and sacrificed it, pouring out its blood upon the altar, and according to legend immediately after the sacrifice he was changed from a man into a wolf (*lycos*). I for my part believe this story.' In the account of the Church Father Clement of Alexandria,

'Lycaon set before [Zeus], as a dainty dish, his [Lycaon's] own child, Nyctimus by name, whom he had slaughtered.' Pliny's *Natural History* 'classes werewolves among persons under a curse', and describes an Arcadian ritual in which a man is taken to a marsh and is there transformed into a wolf for nine years, 'and that if in that period he has refrained from touching a human being, he returns to the same marsh, swims across it, and recovers his shape'. He also recounts the tale of Daemenetus of Parrhasia, who 'tasted the vitals of a boy who had been offered as a [sacrificial] victim and turned himself into a wolf'.

In his *Persian Wars*, the historian Herodotus describes the customs of the Neuri, who lived in what is today Belarus and northern Ukraine, and their neighbours the Man-eaters (*Anthropophagi*), who lived in the region of Scythia (Central Asia):

> It may be that they are wizards; for the Scythians, and the Greeks settled in Scythia, say that once a year every one of the Neuri is turned into a wolf, and after remaining so for a few days returns again to his former shape.... The Man-eaters are of all men the most savage in their manner of life; they know no justice and obey no law. They are nomads, wearing a dress like the Scythians and speaking a language of their own; they are the only people of all there that eat men.

It is difficult to think of a body of mythology or folklore that does not contain narratives of lycanthropy or other forms of beast transformation, and contemporary popular culture is suffused with such narratives. These may originally have emerged from widespread beliefs in types of metempsychosis, the transmigration of souls from one bodily form to another, and might be said to reflect the unity of humanity and nature in a polytheistic order, or even a sense of innate pantheism, in which all living things are divine spirits. Ovid's *Metamorphoses* is in essence an enormous catalogue of such narratives.

Beast transformations of this kind are rarer in monotheistic mythology and theology, much of which emerged from the necessities of harsh desert survival, and thus stresses an essential separation of humanity and nature, which is a force which needs to be mastered and controlled, governed by a series of laws and interdicts, from the Abominations of Leviticus (many of which are dietary) to the Ten Commandments (which emerge out of a period of national survival in the wilderness). One of the few such narratives in the Bible is that of the Babylonian King Nebuchadnezzar, 'deposed from his kingly throne' for his pride and reduced to a life of feral madness: 'And he was driven from the sons of men, and his heart was made like the beasts, and his dwelling *was* with the wild asses; they fed him with grass like oxen, and his body was wet with the dew of heaven' (Daniel 5:20–1). (This is the subject of a famous painting by William Blake, and it has been suggested that Blake drew for this on an illustration of a cannibalistic werewolf by Lucas Cranach; see Figure 5.)

Sometimes lycanthropy is, as Pliny maintained, a straightforward curse, a misfortune brought upon an innocent through sheer bad luck, or as a result of a family history over which they have no control. This remains a significant impetus for modern cinematic lycanthropy, in *Werewolf of London* (1935), *The Wolf Man* (1941), *The Curse of the Werewolf* (1961), or *An American Werewolf in London* (1981). Modern

Figure 5. (a) Lucas Cranach the Elder, *The Werewolf* (*c.*1500–15).

Figure 5. (b) William Blake, *Nebuchadnezzar* (1795).

beast transformations have also found a powerful explanatory narrative in Darwinism, a major source of anxiety ever since the publication of *The Origin of Species* in 1859, as we shall see in Chapter 5. *The Strange Case of Dr Jekyll and Mr Hyde* (1886) and *The Island of Doctor Moreau* (1896) are both explicitly post-Darwinian narratives of beast transformation, and all subsequent tales of lycanthropy are in their different ways necessarily informed by the implication of natural selection that there is no existential division between man and beast.

In many cases, as with Lycaon himself, lycanthropy is both a punishment and a metaphor for savagery. In serving up human flesh (the flesh of a baby; the flesh of his own child) to Zeus, Lycaon violates numerous taboos against blasphemy, unclean eating, familial ties, and the obligations of a host. He transforms into a wolf as an externalization of his own inhumanity. This is very much the interpretation for lycanthropy which the Reverend Sabine Baring-Gould offered in his influential 1865 treatise, *The Book of Were-Wolves*.

Baring-Gould was a kind of super-Victorian, an Anglican clergyman who was also an astoundingly prolific man of letters—a novelist, an antiquary (he wrote *A Book of Dartmoor*, one of Arthur Conan Doyle's sources for *The Hound of the Baskervilles*), a folklorist, a hymnist ('Onward Christian Soldiers'), and much else besides. Baring-Gould's interest in lycanthropy dates, he maintains, from a walking tour in a remote part of Brittany, where he is warned against setting out after dark, for fear of the *loup-garou*, 'a fiend, a worse than fiend, a man-fiend—a worse than man-fiend, a man-wolf-fiend'.

For Baring-Gould, lycanthropy is a moral category. As well as Lycaon himself, Baring-Gould identifies as lycanthropes a number of moral monsters—notorious serial killers and cannibals such as Elizabeth Báthory and Gilles de Rais. He also associates the Berserkers with lycanthropy. These were terrifyingly savage Scandinavian warriors, apparently impervious to pain and injury, who dressed in the skins of beasts for battle: 'The berserkir were said to work themselves into a state of frenzy, in which a demoniacal power came over them, impelling them to acts from which their sober senses would have recoiled . . . and as they rushed into conflict they yelped as dogs or howled as wolves.' Berserker (or 'Bersicker') is the name Bram Stoker chose for the giant wolf that escapes from London Zoo at the Count's bidding in *Dracula*. Dracula commands wolves ('Listen to them—the children of the night. What music they make!'), and is himself a lycanthrope, referred to by the locals as '"Ordog"—Satan, "pokol"—hell, "stregoica"—witch, "vrolok" and "vlkoslak"— both of which mean the same thing, one being Slovak and the other Servian [*sic*] for something that is either werewolf or vampire'. When the Count disembarks the ship he has commandeered, on English soil, he does so in the guise of 'an immense dog', or wolf.

In part because of its association with cannibalism, lycanthropy is also a directly political category, a means of subhumanizing aliens and Others by rendering them as bestial. As we have seen, the further we get from the *polis*, from metropolitan centres of population and civilization— to Colchis, Castle Dracula, the Yorkshire Moors, the Asiatic steppes, Prospero's island, the Island of Doctor Moreau— the closer we get to monstrosity and savagery, as though we are travelling back in time. For Herodotus, the lycanthropic Neuri and their neighbours, the Anthropophagi, lived in remote Eastern Europe and Central Asia. For Pliny, beast-men lived in unexplored Africa:

> Then come regions which are purely imaginary: towards the west are the Nigroi, whose king is said to have only one eye, in his forehead; the Wild-beast-eaters [Agriophagi], who live chiefly on the flesh of panthers and lions; the Eatalls [Pamphagi], who devour everything; the Man-eaters [Anthropophagi], whose diet is human flesh; the Dog-milkers [Cymanolgi], who have dogs' heads; the Arbatitae, who have four legs and rove about like wild animals.

You will notice that Pliny's primary method of taxonomy here is dietary; beast-men are monstrous because they violate food taboos.

Baring-Gould also recognized that lycanthropy was a psychological as well as a moral and geopolitical category. Lycanthropes, he speculated, 'may still prowl in Abyssinian forests, range still over Asiatic steppes, and be found howling dismally in some padded room of a Hanwell or a Bedlam.' The 'zoophagous' R. N. Renfield in *Dracula* was one such lunatic. Another was a patient of Sigmund Freud, Sergei Pankejeff, known as the Wolf Man. Pankejeff suffered from a variety of physical and psychological conditions, and under analysis recounted to Freud a particularly terrifying childhood dream of white wolves sitting in the walnut tree outside his bedroom. Freud interprets this as a displaced rendition of a traumatic episode in which the infant Pankejeff, sleeping in a cot in his parents' bedroom, witnesses a 'Primal Scene', an act of *'coitus a tergo, more ferrarum'* ('sex from behind, like the animals'), allowing him simultaneously to see both parents' genitals, and to interpret his mother's vagina as lack, a castrated bleeding wound. Pankejeff grew into a 'savage' child; for the Wolf Man, Freud concludes, 'the sexual aim could only be cannibalism—devouring'.

The anxious relationship between humanity and wolves is also a recurring trope in folklore, and particularly in the European fairy tale, in which the Big Bad Wolf is a recurring figure. The tale of 'Little Red Riding Hood' is especially ripe for interpretation and adaptation. One of the most widely circulated folktales, 'Little Red Riding Hood' has direct analogues and antecedents that can be traced back to medieval

Europe, and was collected by both Charles Perrault and the Grimm brothers. The tale, with its pubescent heroine and her grandmother, its red cloak, and its rapacious antagonist, is ripe with psychoanalytic suggestion. For the Freudian theorist Bruno Bettelheim in his influential study of fairy tales, *The Uses of Enchantment*, the wolf is 'the male seducer', who 'represents all the asocial, animalistic tendencies within ourselves'. The devouring wolf-grandmother ('What big teeth you have!') who lives in a cottage in the woods has clear links to the cannibalistic witch of the related tale of 'Hansel and Gretel' (also collected by the Grimms). In her feminist study of fairy tales, *From the Beast to the Blonde*, Marina Warner draws together the wolf, the grandmother, and the adolescent girl, as figures linked by their liminality:

> The wolf is kin to the forest-dwelling witch, or crone; he offers us a male counterpart, a werewolf, who swallows up grandmother and then granddaughter. In the witch-hunting fantasies of early modern Europe they are the kind of beings associated with marginal knowledge, who possess pagan secrets and are in turn possessed by them.

Angela Carter's short story collection *The Bloody Chamber* (1979) is one of the most brilliant and important modern collections of fairy tales. The collection returns again and again to versions of 'Little Red Riding Hood', and to the thematically related 'Beauty and the Beast', in its meditations on carnality, animalism, and adolescent female sexuality, and uses the red cloak to symbolize the bleeding vagina of the sexualized female body, in menstruation or loss of virginity: the 'Bloody Chamber' of the title is in part a metaphor for the menstruating womb; the protagonist of 'The Company of Wolves' 'closed her window on the wolves' threnody and took off her scarlet shawl, the colour of poppies, the colour of sacrifices, the colour of her menses'. 'Wolf-Alice', a feral child raised by wolves—'an imperfect wolf'—interprets her first menstruation as the result of being bitten by a wolf who lives in the moon. As a displaced symbol of her impending loss of virginity, the heroine of the title story is given as a wedding gift by her murderous husband 'A choker of rubies, two inches wide, like an extraordinarily precious slit throat.' The bleeding wound of his mother's vagina, which traumatized Freud's Wolf Man, is revisited and reclaimed by Carter throughout the collection, as a source of female power: 'since her fear did her no good', Carter's Little Red Riding Hood decides, 'she ceased to be afraid'.

Carter's influence is very clearly visible on the most important werewolf film of the twenty-first century, John Fawcett's *Ginger Snaps* (2000). Ginger Fitzgerald (Kathryn Isabelle) is bitten by a werewolf on the night of her first period. Her transformation into a lycanthrope is accompanied by heavy menstruation, and in a startling physical realization of her newfound carnality, she develops a voracious sexual appetite and grows a pronounced tail. *Ginger Snaps* is a film about suburban adolescent alienation. Ginger and her sister Brigitte, a pair of nonconformist misfits in their dull Canadian suburb, Bailey Downs, begin the film by fantasizing about suicide, imaginatively depicted in the film's opening photomontage, 'Life in Bailey Downs'. What the 'curse'—of lycanthropy; of the menstruating, sexualized

91

female body—offers *Ginger Snaps*'s teenage protagonist is a way out of the suburbs.

Body Horror

'My mind is bent to tell of bodies changed into new forms.' These are the opening words of Ovid's *Metamorphoses*. Many of the myths recorded by Ovid are graphically *physical* affairs, as in the case of the weaver Arachne's transformation into a spider by Pallas Athena: 'her hair... fell off, and with it both nose and ears; and the head shrank up; her whole body also was small; the slender fingers clung to her side as legs; the rest was belly'.

A significant part of the shock and fascination of horror lies in its attempts to render these transformations convincingly before the audience's very eyes. In 1887, the actor Richard Mansfield stunned theatregoers with his use of photosensitive make-up, which allowed him to transform from Dr Jekyll to Mr Hyde right there on stage (Figure 6). So convincing was this transformation that, the following year, Mansfield briefly found himself a suspect in the ongoing Jack the Ripper investigation, and such was the clamour that he decided to shut the play down. In silent Hollywood, Lon Chaney, 'The Man of a Thousand Faces', underwent extraordinary and often excruciating physical transformations in a number of roles, including Jekyll and Hyde and the Phantom of the Opera. Viewers of *The Wolf Man* got to see Lon Chaney Jr transform into a lycanthrope through the magic of dissolve photography and Jack Pierce's iconic yak hair make-up.

Figure 6. Richard Mansfield transforms from Dr Jekyll to Mr Hyde.

Such cinematic transformations are inevitably technology-driven, and entered a decisively modern phase in the early 1980s, as advances in visual effects and make-up, pioneered by the likes of Rick Baker, Rob Bottin, Tom Savini, and Stan Winston, meant that monstrous transformations could be shown onscreen for the first time in ways that often comprehensively exceeded the power of the audience's imaginations. In *An American Werewolf in London*, Baker's transformation of David Naughton into a wolf, with elongation of limbs and face, cracking of spine, and agonizing screams, is one of the defining moments of modern horror cinema. In Bottin's effects for John Carpenter's *The Thing*, the human body is given a nightmarish plasticity, seemingly able to recombine in any form, as a severed head sprouts spider's legs, Arachne-like, or a huge, fanged gash opens up in a torso, like the very mother of all *vaginae dentatae*. This was the world of 1980s 'body horror', which radically figured, disfigured, and refigured the human body, focusing on it relentlessly as a site of pain, and anxiety and disgust, but also of transformation and transcendence, often with highly sophisticated philosophical and intellectual underpinnings. Body horror of this kind is particularly associated with the work of the Canadian auteur David Cronenberg and the British writer and film-maker Clive Barker.

Consistently across a very distinguished body (corpus) of work, from early low-budget films such as *Shivers* (1975) and *Rabid* (1978), to 1980s classics like *Scanners* (1981), *Videodrome* (1983), or *The Fly* (1986), and beyond the millennium (including his 2014 novel, *Consumed*), Cronenberg has given artistic form to his sense of the human body as a *corporation*, composed of parts which have their own identities and individuality, which they seek to assert, in what is a radical literalizing of mind–body dualism. As a university literature graduate, Cronenberg is also an articulate theorist of his own work:

> I don't think the flesh is necessarily treacherous, evil, bad. It is cantankerous, and it is independent. The idea of independence is the key. It really is like colonialism...I think to myself: 'That's what it is: the independence of the body, relative to the mind, and the difficulty of the mind accepting what that revolution might entail.'

Cronenberg's use of the rhetoric of decolonization here, and his insistence on the relationship between the corporation and the corporeal, suggests a political reading of his work, underlined by his tendency to invent imaginatively named shadowy scientific/commercial organizations (Spectacular Optics, ConSec, the Raglan Institute for Psychoplasmics) which seek to distort and exploit the body for commercial gain. From rapacious capitalism to the AIDS crisis to the 'beauty myth' and its discontents, body horror became an effective means of engaging with and representing the grotesque elements of contemporary lived reality in the 1980s.

The politics of the body are even more to the fore in the work of Clive Barker. Another humanities graduate (English and Philosophy), Barker is, like Cronenberg, a ready theorist of his own work, which he has discussed across numerous, often very candid interviews. Barker, to begin with, is no believer in what was defined in the Introduction as the aesthetics of terror, arising out of implication, restraint, or uncanny uncertainty. There is no fear of the unknown here, and certainly no sense that the reader's or viewer's own imagination should be allowed to conjure the greatest horrors:

> The kind of horror which is all suggestion and undertow, and 'it's what you don't see that horrifies you' kind of stuff—that doesn't do a thing for me. . . . I like imagining horrors in detail. I like to be able to give the reader everything I can imagine on a subject. . . . Horror fiction is about confrontation.

Barker's aesthetic radicalism—his uncompromisingly confident representational style—is matched by a commensurate political radicalism. His best work, the stories collected in the *Books of Blood*, are tales of riotous fleshly mutability, often with an avowedly feminist and/or an openly gay politics. In 'Jacqueline Ess: Her Will and Testament', for example, a bored and frustrated housewife discovers that she has the power to mould flesh, and turns her sexist doctor into a woman:

> She willed his manly chest into making breasts of itself and it began to swell most fetchingly, until the skin burst and his sternum flew apart. His pelvis, teased to breaking point, fractured at its centre . . . It was from between his legs all the noise was coming; the splashing of his blood; the thud of his bowel on the carpet.

Deliberately extreme and often brilliant, Barker's work is a classic example of horror at its most divisive, self-consciously setting out to shock and alienate large sections of the population, while establishing a devoted cult following. As Barker himself maintained:

> I like to think there's some kind of 'celebration of perversity' in the *Books of Blood*. That's a response, simply, to normality.

What I cannot bear is 'normality'. What I'm trying to upset is not something hugely repressive—but something banal, that is, the lives most people lead.

'Torture Porn'

Cronenberg and Barker are exponents of that strain of confrontational, avant-garde horror which we have been discussing throughout the book—a combination of radical aesthetics and politics, and taboo-busting imagery, to a recognizably serious artistic end. But 1980s body horror was also a precursor to a distinctive post-millennial subgenre often called 'torture porn', which concentrates remorselessly on the human body's capacity for pain and suffering, and on the human motives for inflicting that suffering. Torture porn is contemporary horror at its most controversial, since for many viewers and commentators it seems to dispense with body horror's ideological agenda and go straight for its spectacle of the human body in pain: in other words, it is empty sadism. This is certainly an argument that needs engaging with, and I think that, of all forms of horror, torture porn may come closest to realizing the nightmares of hostile critics. Often, indeed, as is the case with Tom Six's *The Human Centipede* (2010), the very *raison d'être* of some torture porn seems to be to bait its critics (and it succeeds!), though some films, most notably Michael Haneke's *Funny Games* (1997), raise serious issues about an audience's enjoyment of pain and suffering, and the role of the entertainment industry in creating or fuelling that enjoyment.

It is important to begin by stressing that the artistic spectacle of the tortured and disfigured human body has long been a major subject of art and culture. The flaying of the piper Marsyas by the god Apollo was a favourite subject of both classical and Renaissance sculpture. Much of the meaning of Christianity derives from the symbolism of torture, of Christ's scourged and crucified body, penetrated through the side by a spear. Mel Gibson's *The Passion of the Christ* (2004) is often justifiably viewed as a work of torture porn, though its images of Christ's broken, bleeding body are inherently no more shocking than Matthias Grünewald's famous depiction of a scarred, emaciated, bleeding Christ on the cross in his Isenheim Altarpiece (*c.*1515), one of the great masterpieces of Christian art. Even a casual reading of *The Golden Legend*, Jacobus de Voragine's influential twelfth-century compendium of the lives and martyrdoms of the saints, will reveal an astonishing catalogue of torture and mutilation. Saint Christina, for example, is martyred by being placed in 'an iron cradle ... fired with oil, pitch, and resin', following which she has her breasts cut off, her tongue cut out, and is finally dispatched with 'two arrows into her heart and one into her side'. Any analysis of torture porn must first take account of the fact its imagery is hardly uniquely modern.

What *is* distinctively contemporary about torture porn is its reaction to and participation in a post-millennial culture of the normalization of torture. Torture porn is part of a broader cultural-political complex of texts, images, and events from the post-9/11 'War on Terror'. These would include, for example, photographs of mistreated prisoners in Abu Ghraib or Guantanamo Bay, media discussions about the ethics and utility of waterboarding as a means of interrogation, and counter-terrorist popular entertainment such as the TV series *24*, which increasingly presented torture as a *first* resort, as Jack Bauer (Kiefer Sutherland) went about his business readily torturing whoever got in his way, including US presidents and members of his own family, all in the name of a supposed greater good. There was, we were informed, a 'ticking bomb' out there, and torture was the only way to reveal its location, saving thousands of lives. However, recent studies have shown that political defences of torture (the 'ticking bomb' argument) are philosophically empty, and that it has no efficacy as a means of gathering information. In 1985, Elaine Scarry's influential book *The Body in Pain* discussed the creation of a theatrical *spectacle* of pain through, for example, the institutions and instruments of torture. Insofar as torture 'works', it does so through spectacle, as a means of spreading (rather than countering) terror, of saying, 'There is literally nothing of which I am not capable. I have no moral limits. Fear me.'

Our pain is inexpressible. Having no straightforward linguistic object, it lies beyond the limits of language, articulable only through imprecise similes (it is like burning, it is like torture, it is like death, it is worse than death), or else non-verbally (we scream, we howl, we cry). In our pain, we are uniquely alone and vulnerable. To exploit this vulnerability, knowingly to inflict extreme pain on others, is to place oneself beyond the boundaries of humanity. In H. G. Wells's *The Island of Doctor Moreau*, a crazed vivisector, who has 'never troubled about the ethics of the matter', is

99

run out of Britain and sets up a laboratory on a remote Pacific island, where he performs surgery without anaesthetic: 'It was as if all the pain in the world had found a voice.' Contemporary reactions to *Moreau* were horrified: the *Review of Reviews* maintained that the novel 'ought never to have been published', and should be withdrawn from circulation; Wells himself believed that it had been received as 'a festival of 'orrors'.

Many of the films that fell foul of the 'video nasties' scandal of the 1980s were certainly disreputable or sleazy (*Cannibal Holocaust, I Spit on Your Grave*), but they were generally low-budget affairs, often characterized by a manic energy and a certain DIY integrity. Part of the mystique of these films was the challenge of getting to see them in the first place—they rarely had theatrical runs, and could be difficult to find in video libraries. These were films which had no desire to be mainstream. One of the most disturbing things about modern torture porn is its corporatization. The *Hostel* and *Saw* franchises were mass-distribution multiplex releases. As a Japanese client says of the torture company in Eli Roth's *Hostel* (2005), 'Be careful. You could spend *all* your money in there.' It is difficult to know whether this is critique or celebration.

4

Horror and the Mind

In Chapter 3, we looked at internal threats, at the location of horror within ourselves, in our own bodies and their capacity for metamorphosis or their status as a site of pain. But many of us would consider our minds to be the true location of our sense of identity and individuality, and so internal horror has naturally tended to destabilize this belief, to present the mind as a site of uncertainty. We might be strangers to ourselves, or subject to psychological forces beyond our control. The minds of others may be radically unavailable to us: ineffable, totally devoid of empathy, utterly malignant, or simply blank. These are terrifying ideas, ripe for exploration in horror. Romano Scavolini's *Nightmares in a Damaged Brain* (1981) was an ultra-controversial 'video nasty' banned under the 1984 Video Recordings Act; the film's British distributor, David Grant, was sentenced to eighteen months' imprisonment for releasing an uncut copy. While certainly shoddy, exploitative, and unpleasant, the film is inherently no worse than many others in circulation at the time. What ultimately distinguished Scavolini's film, I believe, was its truly disturbing *title*.

Madness haunts horror, embodied in the figure of the lunatic, the psychopath, or the split personality. One influential tendency of modern thinking about psychiatric disorders, as exemplified by the work of the historical theorist Michel Foucault or the radical clinician R. D. Laing, is to understand madness as a social or political problem rather than a medical one. Madness is a category, a name given to various forms of socially disruptive or threatening ideas and behaviours, and thus a means of regulating undesirable behaviour and of controlling it through institutions of power and of coercion—the medical profession, psychiatry, the asylum.

Horror is often sceptical of this radical social reading of madness, in a manner analogous to the way in which, as we saw in Chapter 1, it does not subscribe to the liberal 'man-eating myth' interpretation of cannibalism. In horror, madness tends to be an existential category of radical Otherness, even or especially when this Other is also ourself. Dr Sam Loomis (Donald Pleasence), the psychiatrist who has spent the better part of a career attempting to treat Michael Myers in John Carpenter's *Halloween*, is the very antithesis of R. D. Laing. Years of studying Michael have convinced Loomis that he is straightforwardly the embodiment of evil; when Michael escapes from the asylum, Loomis follows him to Haddonfield, gun in hand, as the only solution is to kill him. Horror's fascination with madness is often markedly anti-liberal, at odds with progressive modernity. We cannot cure madness, let alone understand it—least of all, like R. D. Laing, embrace it. We can imprison the mad, or we can destroy them, before they destroy us.

But this is a very simplistic view, both of madness and of horror. The practice of the representation of madness in horror can be more nuanced, often turning on the problematic, undecideable relationship between 'madness' and 'normality'. The clear boundary between these states is the very one the asylum and psychiatric pathologizing exists to police. 'They' are mad because 'They' are institutionalized and treated. I am not in an asylum, therefore I am 'sane', normal. But as we have seen many times, horror probes at the weaknesses of such boundaries, breaking them down, troubling our certainties. Beneath the conformist, placid, courteous, deferential, appealing exterior of *Psycho*'s Norman Bates lies a tangled complex of taboos and cracked binaries: living/dead; male/female; mother/son; mother/lover; straight/queer; self/other.

The psychiatric institution, lunatic asylum, madhouse, or bedlam is one of the great recurring locations of horror, and its narratives often turn on ambiguity, the difficulty in distinguishing madness from sanity. From Wilkie Collins's *The Woman in White* onwards, we have narratives of sane people committed to asylums for nefarious reasons, or because their behaviour defies social convention, or simply because they are, in the title of Sarah Wise's study of Victorian lunacy, 'inconvenient people'. A significant amount of the action of Bram Stoker's *Dracula* takes place in Dr Seward's mental institution, where Renfield's episodes of unclean eating are punctuated by moments of startling lucidity. It is possible that the entirety of the action of Robert Wiene's foundational horror film, the intensely political *The Cabinet of Dr. Caligari* (1919), takes place within the confines of an asylum, or that, for this film, the whole world may be mad. Often, protagonists or narrators who gain our trust and sympathy, or who appear to have narrative authority, are finally revealed as lunatics. The great Peter Cushing specialized in such roles, from the appalling Baron Frankenstein in *Frankenstein and the Monster from Hell* (1974) to the crazed, vulnerable anthropologist of *The Creeping Flesh* (1973). Cushing is also one of the inmates in *Asylum* (1972), a portmanteau collection of stories by Robert Bloch (the author of *Psycho*), and a film whose framing narrative turns on the challenge of diagnosing the 'incurably insane'. *Asylum* is also the title of the lauded second season (2012–13) of *American Horror Story*, whose episodes attempt to diagnose the fractured history and pathology of the apparent 1960s serial killer Kit Walker (Evan Peters).

'Madman!'

Madness is the dominant subject of one of the greatest of all horror writers. In the work of Edgar Allan Poe, we return again and again to the figure of the madman, utterly enclosed in the internal world of his (the protagonists are almost always male) own mind. 'True!—nervous—very, very dreadfully nervous I had been and am; but why *will* you say that I am mad?' This opening sentence of 'The Tell-Tale Heart' draws explicit attention to what is a recurring feature of Poe's stories: the variety of obsessions, monomanias, and morbid nervous conditions under which their narrators labour.

Poe famously believed that 'the death...of a beautiful woman is, unquestionably, the most poetical topic in the world, and equally it is beyond doubt that the lips best suited for such topic are those of a bereaved lover'. Egaeus, the narrator of 'Berenice', suffers from a 'monomania... [which] consisted in a morbid irritability of those properties of the mind in metaphysical science termed the *attentive*'. Monomania is the fixation on one idea to the point of madness, and here Egaeus's madness takes the form of an obsession with his beloved cousin Berenice's teeth. After her death, he breaks into her coffin and pulls them out.

The imprisoning sense of interiority makes Poe's narrators highly unreliable: part of the fascination of Poe's stories is that they are so unsettlingly monologic—that is, they have only one voice, only one perspective. In 'Ligeia', the obsessed, grief-stricken narrator believes that his dead wife, Ligeia, has, through the unconquerable force of her will, possessed the body of his second wife, Rowena. The reader simply has no way of judging the reality of this narrative. In 'The Fall of the House of Usher', there does at least seem to be an external perspective on events, as the tale is narrated by an old school friend of Roderick Usher. Once again, Usher suffers from a 'mental disorder', 'a constitutional and family evil' characterized by 'a morbid acuteness of the senses'. His narcoleptic sister Madeleine is buried alive, and disinters herself from her tomb, as Roderick cries, '*Madman! I tell you she now stands without the door!*' Who is the 'Madman' here? Is it Roderick or the narrator? The reader has no way of knowing, and so yet again no way of accounting for the provenance or the veracity of the story.

Following in the tradition of Poe, 'madness' in horror has often been a spectacular, florid, performative affair, and a certain strain of horror madman is characterized by raging egomania, grandiose gestures and grandiloquent rhetoric, and a particular fondness for organ-playing. Often, he has advanced medical or academic qualifications, as though driven mad by intellectual brilliance: Dr Caligari, Dr X, Dr Moreau, Dr Frankenstein, Dr Phibes, Dr Lecter. Hannibal Lecter is, in fact, the major contemporary exemplar of this type of Poe-inflected madness: in his practice as a psychiatrist, he is about as far removed from R. D. Laing as you can get, and certainly no subscriber to the idea of the man-eating myth.

In part, Anthony Hopkins seems to have based his iconic, Oscar-winning portrayal of Lecter on the screen persona of Vincent Price, who made his reputation as a horror star in a series of Roger Corman-directed Poe adaptations for American International Pictures in the 1960s. Musing on Hopkins's portrayal of Lecter in *The Silence of the Lambs* (1991) and his own in *Manhunter* (1986), the actor Brian Cox suggested that 'the difference between Anthony Hopkins's performance and mine is that Tony Hopkins is mad and I am insane!' Cox is on to something with this observation, counterpointing Hopkins's grandstanding performance with his own relatively understated one. At the actual opposite end of the scale of performative madness from Poe, Price, and Hopkins are the various lunatic killers of the 1980s slasher movie—Michael Myers, Jason Voorhees, and their kin, who often have no motivation whatsoever beyond motiveless, unindividuated destructiveness. These psychopathic killers trouble us because they have too little personality, not too much.

The Double

Etymologically, 'individuality' means that which cannot be divided: we are indivisible, at one with ourselves. Much psychological horror has worked hard to destabilize this secure sense of the unified self through its presentation of doppelgängers, twins, shadows, mirrors, portraits, repetitions, madwomen in the attic, and other forms of doubling and fracturing. Many of the great works of nineteenth-century horror are tales of the double: *Frankenstein*, *Confessions of a Justified Sinner*, 'William Wilson', *Dr Jekyll and Mr Hyde*, *The Picture of Dorian Gray*. The split personality, the evil twin, the double life, the cursed mirror, the living statue, the changing portrait, the return of the repressed, the cycle of events across generations, the dream which infects or overwhelms reality. These narratives and themes, all suggestive of the uncanny possibility that we are not at home with ourselves, or that our lives are being lived elsewhere, are all familiar ones in horror culture.

The idea of the double has understandably preoccupied psychoanalysis, and in this context has its origins in the pioneering work of Freud and Otto Rank. Both Freud and Rank suggest that the figure of the double was originally a religious one, expressive of the sense of the duality of body and soul. If our double is originally the embodiment of our soul, then it follows that an encounter with the double should portend death, that moment when body and soul are finally divided. Paradoxically, then, the double, originally an embodiment of our immortality, is also a reminder of the mortality of our own bodies. An encounter with the double is a rupture in time and space, a moment when the world of matter and the world of spirit, this life and the afterlife, meet.

In Mary Shelley's novel, Victor Frankenstein builds a creature out of dead tissue, animating it with a spark of life, as a means of discovering human immortality through the overmastering power of Enlightenment science. The Monster's threat to Victor Frankenstein, 'I will be with you on your wedding night', can be read in a number of ways. Victor interprets the threat as meaning, 'I [the Monster] am coming to get you [Victor] on your wedding night.' The events of the novel suggest that it means, 'I am coming to get your bride on your wedding night.' But it can very plausibly be interpreted as meaning, 'I will be your bride'—as any viewer of *The Rocky Horror Picture Show* will recognize.

The double, I have suggested, can signify the death of the self, but it can also signify narcissism, morbid self-love. In Greek myth, when the beautiful Narcissus gazed upon his reflection in the pool, he was so entranced by his own beauty that he could not look away, and so he withered and died (or in some versions threw himself into the pool and drowned). The concept of narcissism as a psychoanalytic pathology was first formulated in the last years of the nineteenth century by the sexologist Henry Havelock Ellis and the psychiatrist Paul Näcke, who coined the phrase 'Narcismus'. For both Havelock Ellis and Näcke, narcissism essentially meant masturbation (sex with someone you love, as Woody Allen put it). Rank and Freud both wrote important studies of narcissism, broadening the term to denote a variety of megalomania in which attention cannot be redirected from the self to others: 'The libido that has been withdrawn from the external world has been directed to the ego and thus gives rise to an attitude which may be called narcissism', Freud wrote.

This sense of the divided, narcissistic personality as representing egomania, or even megalomania, is certainly important to the nineteenth-century double narrative, as particularly exemplified in the figure of Dorian Gray, whose astonishing beauty captivates all who see him, and who essentially switches place with his own portrait, which records the corrupting traces of narcissism upon his soul. The narcissistic double continues into the twentieth century and beyond in figures as otherwise different from one another as Norman Bates (who is also his own mother) and *Fight Club*'s Tyler Durden: David Fincher's 1999 adaptation of Chuck Palahniuk's novel brilliantly exploits Brad Pitt's extraordinarily narcissistic screen persona for this role. The theme of the narcissistic double also animates Darren Aronofsky's *Black Swan* (2010), in Nina's (Natalie Portman) psychosexual relationships with her own apparent doppelgänger, and with her rival and counterpart Lily (Mila Kunis).

As well as a pathological psychoanalytic condition, the divided self is also (and sometimes at the same time) a potent literary and cultural symbol. It can, for example, represent a divided national identity. Scottish writers such as James Hogg (*Confessions of a Justified Sinner*), Robert Louis

Stevenson (*Dr Jekyll and Mr Hyde*), and Arthur Conan Doyle ('The Winning Shot') have made significant contributions to the literature of the double, as have Irish writers such as Oscar Wilde (*The Picture of Dorian Gray*). In all these cases, a national 'double consciousness' underlies these narratives, sometimes problematizing their official political positions and statements.

This, as we saw in the Introduction, is emphatically the case with Conan Doyle, a man much given to hyper-confident statements of belief in the moral mission of the British Empire, who twice stood for Parliament as a Unionist, was explicitly opposed to Irish Home Rule, but who was himself not only Scottish, but a Scotsman of Catholic Irish parentage, whose fiction revealed an altogether more troubled, divided figure. In his work, the English genius Sherlock Holmes, who uncovers meaning and upholds order, is countered and matched by the Irish genius Professor Moriarty, who works in secret and spreads chaos. They are like the conscious and the unconscious minds. Conan Doyle's long and distinguished public career brought this Unionist Edinburgh physician into contact not only with mediums and spiritualists, as we have seen, but also with Irish nationalists and revolutionaries: Roger Casement and Erskine Childers, both of whom lost their lives in the cause of Irish independence. In the end, these contradictions were to prove too much for Conan Doyle. His father, Charles Altamont Doyle, was an artist and illustrator who specialized in pictures of fairies. A psychologically tormented man, he spent his last years as an inmate of a lunatic asylum. A young doctor being summoned to care for a genteel, older lunatic is a recurring narrative in Conan Doyle's fiction, in the short stories 'The Surgeon of Gaster Fell' and 'The Beetle-Hunter' (in which a distinguished aristocratic entomologist has episodes of homicidal lunacy), and in his autobiographical novel *The Stark-Munro Letters* (1895). Conan Doyle spent his own last years insisting on the reality of fairies, as he took up the case of the Cottingley fairy photographs (obvious fakes) with his usual confident assurance, an episode which destroyed his public reputation.

The doppelgänger can also embody the double life, whether this is a case of hypocrisy (the 'double standard' of public virtue and private vice) or the enforced concealment of sexual identities. Both of these elements play significant roles in *The Strange Case of Dr Jekyll and Mr Hyde*, the archetypal narrative of the double. Stevenson's 1886 novella takes place entirely within a world of men—specifically, the repressed, respectable, professional world of Jekyll himself, and of his friends Utterson, a lawyer, Lanyon, a doctor, and Enfield, 'the well-known man about town'.

The fact that this is a 'strange case' implies both a medical and a legal narrative, and Jekyll's friends hint that Hyde may be the result of Jekyll's 'wild' youth come back to haunt him; Jekyll himself acknowledges that in his youth, 'my pleasures were (to say the least) undignified', that he is prone to 'appetites which I had long secretly indulged and had of late begun to pamper'. Hyde is a much younger man than Jekyll, and also a lower-class man. It is strongly implicit in the text that Jekyll's friends believe Hyde to be some kind of 'rough trade', a working-class East Ender with whom the genteel, West End Jekyll is having an illicit gay relationship,

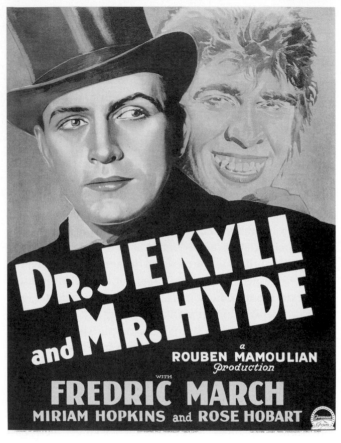

Figure 7. Fredric March as Dr Jekyll and Mr Hyde (1931).

whom he has moved into his London townhouse and is financially keeping, or who is blackmailing him. Only in later, cinematic iterations, often strongly influenced by the Jack the Ripper story, does Hyde explicitly become a hetero-sexual sex-killer, and Jekyll's 'undignified' pleasures a predilection for prostitutes. Fredric March's Oscar-winning 1931 performance in the title role goes down the full path of moral and evolutionary degeneration, turning the upright Jekyll into a gleefully sadistic, simian sex-maniac (Figure 7). But whatever the exact nature of Jekyll's 'appetites', their socialized repression has twisted and pathologized them, transforming Eros into Thanatos, desire into violence. As Jekyll himself says of Hyde, 'My devil had long been caged, he came out roaring.'

Psychos and Slashers: The Serial Killer

The serial killer is our great modern demon. This figure is a source of recurring fascination in horror, and in popular culture at large. A glance at the 'True Crime' shelves of any bookshop will reveal dozens of pop-biographical and quasi-criminological 'studies' of notorious serial killers and their unspeakable crimes. Peter Sutcliffe, Ted Bundy, Dennis Nilsen, John Wayne Gacy, Fred and Rosemary West, Jeffrey Dahmer, Henry Lee Lucas, Harold Shipman. We repeat their names as a litany of fear. Often, supernatural power or superhuman genius is ascribed to these figures, generally in direct antithesis to historical reality. Hannibal Lecter, as Thomas Harris's later novels strongly imply, may well be the

Devil himself, a figure of vast learning, intellect, and culture who seems to act out of an authentic sense of categorical species superiority, but real-life serial killers tend on the whole to be poorly educated social misfits. If realism is the aim, then the grim and downbeat *Henry: Portrait of a Serial Killer* (1990), which drew on the crimes of the drifter Henry Lee Lucas, is a truer representation of serial killers than the hyperbolic *The Silence of the Lambs*.

Serial killer horror is a genre distinctive to modernity. It grows out of the urban experience. Patrick Bateman, the murderous protagonist of Bret Easton Ellis's *American Psycho*, is a product if not an embodiment of 1980s New York. Even when the killers are rural or provincial, as in *Psycho*, *The Texas Chain Saw Massacre*, or *Wolf Creek*, their victims are typically urbanites gone astray, off the beaten path, taking the wrong turn.

Most specifically, serial killer horror reflects anxieties about the anonymity of city life: Kevin Spacey's killer in *Se7en*, for example, is the very embodiment of this anonymity—his only name is 'John Doe'. While there are always antecedents, the modern serial killer's origins are in the nineteenth century. London was the first modern megacity, growing exponentially with the British Empire across the nineteenth century to become not just the biggest city in the world, but far and away the biggest city in the history of the world.

> Then the vision of an enormous town presented itself, of a monstrous town more populous than some continents and in its man-made might as if indifferent to heaven's frowns

and smiles; a cruel devourer of the world's light. There was room enough to place any story, depth enough for any passion, variety enough there for any setting, darkness enough to bury five millions of lives.

Here, Joseph Conrad's account of the genesis of *The Secret Agent* gives some sense of the endless possibilities and limitless terror of *fin-de-siècle* London. Sherlock Holmes was created to make reassuring sense of this boundless complexity, but for most observers the city's fog and numberless streets could conceal monsters: Mr Hyde, Count Dracula, Professor Moriarty, Fu Manchu. Perhaps the most terrifying of all of these was Jack the Ripper, whose unsolved, extraordinarily gruesome murders still haunt the cultural imagination: every year, it seems, some new iteration of the events or some 'definitive' proof of the Ripper's identity will appear.

It is this very lack of a definitive identity—the fact that he could have been anyone—that is at the heart of Jack the Ripper's enduring fascination. One of Edgar Allan Poe's strangest and most inconclusive tales is called 'The Man of the Crowd'. The story's narrator, a London *flâneur* and man about town, becomes fascinated and horrified, for reasons he cannot articulate, by a figure he sees among the throng of lawyers, merchants, clerks, and criminals that make up the metropolitan scene. He follows the man—who carries a dagger and wears a diamond ring—through the 'thick humid fog' of the London evening, from the city's busy squares to its squalid suburban gin palaces. The narrator comes to realize that what is horrifying about the 'Man of the Crowd' is not the man but the crowd. He is faceless, nameless, and yet disturbing because he is the embodiment of the city, there wherever people are. This may be one of Poe's tales of the double: the narrator himself, who wanders the packed streets at night, is no less 'The Man of the Crowd'. Poe's story was first published in 1840, and sets the template for the representation of unsettling urban anonymity.

We are in this anonymous London in one of the foundational works of contemporary serial killer culture, Michael Powell's *Peeping Tom* (1960). Karl Boehm's Mark, the killer of the film, is good-looking but bland, shy, and socially awkward, and, importantly for the action of the film, he lives in a house divided into apartments. *Peeping Tom* is fascinating on a number of levels. Famously, it is a rebarbative meditation by a major English director on the voyeurism and sadism of film-making. Mark is a photographer and film-maker: he films the deaths of his female victims, whom he kills with a spike attached to his camera. Powell himself plays Mark's father, who conducted sadistic psychological experiments on him as a child. The house, in which Mark appears to be a tenant, is actually his father's house, now divided into separate apartments—a symbol of the fractured self.

In its depiction of isolated, sexually vulnerable murder victims in anonymous rented rooms—people who would not be missed preyed on by people you would not notice— the film spoke powerfully to post-war Britain (too powerfully, in fact, as the film received savagely negative reviews, and effectively ended Powell's career as a film-maker in Britain). The year previously, in November 1959, the *New Yorker* published 'The Landlady', a story by Roald Dahl, reprinted the following year as the opening tale in his third collection of short stories, *Kiss Kiss*. In the story, seventeen-year-old Billy Weaver moves to Bath to start his first job, and takes a room in a guest house run by a seemingly kindly landlady with a passion for taxidermy, which she practises on her tenants, after giving them poisoned tea: 'There wasn't a *blemish* on his body.... His skin was *just* like a baby's.'

On 21 April 1979, 'The Landlady' was memorably adapted as part of the first season of *Tales of the Unexpected*, a long-running series of dramatizations of macabre stories, initially all by Dahl. This went a good deal further than Dahl's original story, in closing with shots of the stuffed bodies of previous tenants, lying in bed in their room. Dahl's land-lady shares with Norman Bates a passion for taxidermy, a tendency to view living things as objects. The motel, the boarding house, the bedsit, the furnished room—these house transient, unstable, untraceable populations, and are also themselves symbolic of the divided mind, the person-ality not at home with itself. With its strong implications of necrophilia, the TV adaptation 'The Landlady' has clear parallels with the contemporaneous activities of Dennis Nilsen. Nilsen was an apparently unremarkable, bland civil servant who between 1978 and 1983 took at least twelve men back to his flats in the unremarkable, bland London suburbs of Cricklewood and Muswell Hill, where he mur-dered them and kept their bodies with him at home, some-times for months on end.

Like the Gothic castle, the Old Dark House, the cabin in the woods, or the hotel, the suburbs are one of the arche-typal locations of horror. Especially in the post-war decades, this reflects the fact that the suburbs are where much of the audience for horror actually tended to live. Popular culture has always had an ambivalent relationship with this fact. When H. G. Wells's Martians came to wreak their holocaust upon the earth in *The War of the Worlds*, it was the very south London suburbs in which Wells himself lived that they destroyed first. A significant part of the power of *Halloween*, the film which effectively began the modern slasher movie phenomenon, lies in its suburban setting, as the escaped lunatic Michael Myers 'comes home' to Haddonfield, Illinois.

Michael Myers is utterly anonymous. He has no personality at all, and no motivation. He is not, in any way that we recognize, an individual. He does not have a face, or at least not one that we ever see—Michael is the first of the many mask-wearing psychos of modern horror, and his is a white, expressionless mask. (Famously, John Carpenter adapted a William Shatner mask for Michael, but that's another story.) Dressed in work overalls, he could be a maintenance man, come to fix your boiler. Michael Myers is a fact of suburban life, precisely the kind of person who could move unseen through a suburb like Haddonfield.

To no less a degree than the fugue, the villanelle, the romcom, the ghost story, or the power ballad, the slasher movie is a formal aesthetic exercise governed by a strict narrative grammar. The psycho returns on the anniversary of a past misdeed (this is why calendars and holidays are so important to the slasher movie: *Halloween*, *Friday the 13th*, *Prom Night*, *My Bloody Valentine*, *Happy Birthday to Me*, *Silent Night, Deadly Night*, and many others). A group of teens are bloodily dispatched with sharp implements, often in a manner directly related to their sexual activity. A 'final girl', often nonsexual and with a gender-indeterminate name (Laurie, Marti, Terry, Stretch, Sidney), survives to thwart and destroy the killer, at least temporarily. As we have seen throughout this study, the ritualistic element of horror is very important, and the slasher movie represents horror at its most ritualistic. The slasher movie is barely peopled by 'characters' at all, but rather by narrative functions and agents, all acting out predetermined roles.

The cinematic figure of the psycho troubles one particular categorical boundary, that between human and non-human. Does he (they are almost always male) belong to a secular, materialist ontology (where madness is a social problem, where it can be treated by psychiatric intervention), or does he belong to a supernatural order? In their indestructibility and seeming omnipresence, the archetypal slashers, Michael Myers and Jason Voorhees, were essentially supernatural monsters, creatures of nightmare—a premise carried further by the appearance of an unambiguously supernatural figure, Freddy Krueger, protagonist of the long-running *Nightmare on Elm Street* series, and himself only the most high-profile of a number of contemporaneous dream-demons, in films such as *Phantasm* (1979) and *Dreamscape* (1984).

The very space occupied by the slasher—the suburban home—became uncanny by his presence, as time and space cracked and expanded: basements and bedrooms became labyrinths, and even in a modest home, no one could hear you scream. As I have suggested, by the publication of *Hannibal* (1999) even Thomas Harris seems unsure as to whether

Dr Lecter is actually the Devil. By the close of the third TV season of *Hannibal* (2015), the series had become highly surreal, heavily influenced by David Lynch and Dario Argento. The confines of realism, that great literary form of rational modernity, could no longer contain Lecter, who carries within him another world.

5

Science and Horror

In 1995, the year before his death, the distinguished astronomer and science writer Carl Sagan published a book entitled *The Demon-Haunted World*. Subtitled *Science as a Candle in the Dark*, the book had its origins in a course Sagan taught at Cornell University, 'Critical thinking in scientific and non-scientific contexts'. *The Demon-Haunted World* is an analysis of the follies, but also the temptations, of occult thinking and pseudoscience, which offer misleading or simplistic, if sometimes emotionally satisfying, answers to complex questions. Sagan was no philistine—he was the most polymathically humanistic of public intellectuals, with a real understanding of the power of myth, the importance of religion, the necessity of art. But he was acutely aware of the cultural and intellectual deficit that results from scientific ignorance. Without some understanding of and sympathy for science, intellectual citizenship was under threat, and with that the very possibility of educating a responsible electorate.

In part, Sagan realized, scientific illiteracy arose out of a climate of distrust. This was understandable:

> Our technology has produced thalidomide, CFCs, Agent
> Orange, nerve gas, pollution of air and water, species extinc-
> tions, and industries so powerful they can ruin the climate of
> our planet. Roughly half the scientists on Earth work at least
> part-time for the military . . . . There's a *reason* people are ner-
> vous about science.

This fear and distrust of science and scientists is a major
component of modern horror. In part, this is an aspect of
horror's suspicion towards authority, in this case the overwhelming claims made for science as the *only* explanatory
model, the only approach to existence worth taking
seriously, the only method that matters. As we saw in
Chapter 4, scientific genius is often understood in horror as
a dangerous species of madness. Victor Frankenstein is only
the most famous of a large group of unethical experimentalists
in bloodstained laboratory coats, scalpel or serum in hand, or
else of bloodless, abstract theoreticians who would, like
Edward Teller, destroy the world in order to satisfy their intellectual curiosity. *Fiat experimentum in corpore vili* ('Let the
experiment be performed on a worthless corpse'). The attitude
expressed in this Latin proverb informs much of the anxiety
horror has about science, the fear people have of being
treated as *corpora vilia*, expendable experimental subjects.

This kind of anti-scientific popular culture is a fundamentally modern affair, and in essence dates from the climate of
scientific materialism which followed in the wake of the
publication of *The Origin of Species* in 1859. The term 'scientific materialism' was coined in 1872 by the Irish physicist
John Tyndall; T. H. Huxley, Charles Darwin's colleague, pre-
ferred the term 'scientific naturalism', which he understood

as antithetical to 'supernaturalism'. Tyndall and Huxley were at the centre of a group of Victorian scientists who challenged the cultural and intellectual authority of the Church of England, one important battle in a broader Victorian 'crisis of faith'. Famously, Huxley debated evolution with Bishop Samuel Wilberforce in the Oxford University Natural History Museum on 30 June 1860, a debate which history, at least, judged Huxley to have won by knockout when he answered Wilberforce's snide question 'was it through his grandfather or grandmother that he claimed descent from a monkey?' with the answer that 'He was not ashamed to have a monkey for an ancestor; but he would be ashamed to be connected with a man who used great gifts to obscure the truth.' Huxley recognized that evolution's dethroning of humanity from the pinnacle of creation was psychologically and existentially shocking, causing 'the awakening of a sudden and profound mistrust of time-honoured theories and strongly-rooted prejudices regarding [humanity's] own position in nature'.

Huxley taught evolutionary biology to H. G. Wells in what is now Imperial College in London. Wells acknowledged that his intellectual debt to Huxley was immeasurable, and it can be seen very clearly in his own Darwinist horror, *The Island of Doctor Moreau*, in which a crazed vivisector attempts to demonstrate the relationship between man and beast by transforming a variety of animals into human beings. These concerns about the status and place of humanity raised by scientific materialism in general and Darwinism in particular are anxieties with which horror continues to wrestle, because culture at large does. 'Mad science'—scientific progress completely severed from any ethical concerns—is a recurring trope in horror, and can be understood as giving form to genuine concerns about unchecked technological progress and its potential for dehumanization.

Mad Science

Carl Sagan's enumeration of some of the reasons we have for being 'nervous about science' leads to a description of one of the products of that nervousness embodied in a familiar figure:

> And so the image of the mad scientist haunts our world— down to the white-coated loonies of Saturday morning TV and the plethora of Faustian bargains in popular culture, from the eponymous Dr. Faustus himself to *Dr. Frankenstein*, *Dr. Strangelove*, and *Jurassic Park*.

In this section, we will look at a number of these popular cultural manifestations of mad science. We will begin, as Sagan does, with 'the eponymous Dr. Faustus himself'.

In 1528, Johann (or possibly Georg) Faust was driven out of the German university town of Ingolstadt, accused of alchemy. Much is uncertain about his life (not least the fact that there seem to have been two different near-contemporary Fausts, Johann and Georg), but he seems to have been an alchemist, astrologer, magician, and author of numerous *grimoires*, or spell-books. According to contemporary accounts, Faust 'dares to call himself the prince of necromancers, [but] is a vagrant, a charlatan, and a rascal'. Faust was a fairly well-known figure during his lifetime, certainly notorious enough to have attracted the notice of Reformation leaders and intellectuals such as Martin Luther and Philip Melanchthon. In 1540 or 1541, he blew himself up at an inn in Staufen while experimenting with chemicals; the whiff of sulphur left behind was a sure sign that he had been claimed by the Devil, there to make good on their deal and claim his soul. After his death, a number of legends began to attach themselves to Faust, whose exploits began to be recorded in a number of widely circulated works, including the anonymous *Faustbuch*, the *Historia von D. Johann Fausten*, published by Johann Spies in Frankfurt in 1587.

An English translation of this *Faustbuch* was a major source for Christopher Marlowe's *The Tragical History of the Life and Death of Doctor Faustus* (*c.*1604). Marlowe's Faustus is the most brilliant scholar of his generation. Frustrated at having hit the limits of human knowledge, he sells his soul to the Devil in order to 'Resolve me of all ambiguities'. He conducts the kind of black magic ritual we saw in Chapter 2, an inversion of traditional religious rites: 'Within this circle is Jehova's name | Forward and backward anagrammatised.' Marlowe's Faustus is a character distinctive of modernity, the scientist willing to transgress all human and moral limits in the search for knowledge.

Goethe's version of the Faust story (published in two parts, 1808 and 1832) turned it into a fable of Enlightenment scientific and philosophical advancement, even going so far as to save Faust's soul, which is led into heaven at the close of Part II. It was Goethe's version that Mary Shelley knew; she read a commentary on Part I before starting work on *Frankenstein*. Victor Frankenstein, popular culture's archetypal brilliant, overreaching mad scientist, is a student at Ingolstadt, which had banished Faust himself in 1528, and whose university had more recently been the birthplace of the Order of the Illuminati. This was a secret society of anti-clerical freethinkers founded in 1776 by the university's Professor of Canon Law and Philosophy, Adam Weishaupt, and outlawed (along with all other Bavarian secret societies) in 1785.

Frankenstein predates the absolute division between the scientific and occult worlds of the later nineteenth century, and so Victor himself is meant to be understood as an Illuminatus or a Rosicrucian, both a magus and a scientist. His initial intellectual inspiration comes from reading the alchemical writings of Cornelius Agrippa, Albertus Magnus, and Paracelsus, from whom he gets ideas about black magic: 'The raising of ghosts or devils was a promise liberally accorded by my favourite authors.' Although his formal scientific training at Ingolstadt displaces the methods of the alchemists, it does not remove their aims: 'I had a contempt for the uses of modern natural philosophy. It was very different when the masters of the science taught immortality and power; such views, although futile, were grand.' Victor Frankenstein is a scientific necromancer; he raises the dead. *Frankenstein* is particularly preoccupied with the deaths of women and children, and with a masculinist desire for a kind of supreme phallus, doing away with the necessity of women for procreation. In a remarkably sexually invasive metaphor, Victor's chemistry professor, Waldman, describes the advances of Enlightenment scientists: 'They penetrate into the recesses of nature, and shew how she works in her hiding places.'

Frankenstein is subtitled *The Modern Prometheus*. The myth of the Titan Prometheus exists in a number of related forms. In one early version, to be found in Hesiod's *Theogony* (*c.*700 BC), Prometheus steals fire from the gods to give to man, thus in essence bringing about human culture. Prometheus, according to Robert Graves's gloss of the myth, was learned in 'architecture, astronomy, mathematics, navigation, metallurgy and other useful arts, which he passed on to mankind'. In later iterations, as in Ovid's *Metamorphoses*, Prometheus is the *creator* of mankind, whom he moulds from clay, since 'the new earth, but lately drawn away from heavenly ether, still retains some elements of its kindred sky'. In all cases, Prometheus is punished by the gods for his transgression: chained to a rock in the Caucasus, an eagle eats his liver every day, only for it to grow back, the cycle of torment repeating endlessly.

The Prometheus myth, then, simultaneously warns of the dangers of forbidden knowledge (the stolen fire) and insists that knowledge, creativity, and human civilization itself are all transgressive acts. In the quest for knowledge, the Promethean disregards social norms, which are constraints (the chains) punitively enforced (the eagle). For the Romantics of Mary Shelley's generation, Prometheus was a heroic figure; in an age of revolutions, he was the first revolutionary. The Devil was read as a revolutionary Promethean, rebelling against God's autocratic rule. In his classic rereading of John Milton's *Paradise Lost* against the grain of its author's ostensible intentions, William Blake famously wrote in *The*

Marriage of Heaven and Hell that 'The reason Milton wrote in fetters when he wrote of Angels & God, and at liberty when of Devils & Hell, is because he was a true Poet and of the Devil's party without knowing it.' When, in his poem 'The Tyger', Blake asked, 'On what wings dare he aspire? | What the hand dare seize the fire?', he was consciously invoking the stolen fire of the Prometheus myth. The Greek tragedian Aeschylus had dramatized the Prometheus myth in *Prometheus Bound* and its sequel *Prometheus Unbound*, which exists only in fragmentary forms. Percy Bysshe Shelley, classically educated at Eton and Oxford, recast Aeschylus for his own *Prometheus Unbound* (1820), a highly symbolic poetic articulation of his own revolutionary democratic beliefs. This is the intellectual climate out of which *Frankenstein*, very much a novel of ideas, emerges.

Frankenstein itself is ambivalent about its Promethean transgressor, and about his creation. The novel variously renders Victor Frankenstein as an unethical experimenter, a grave robber, a neglectful husband, and a deadbeat dad. The Monster himself speaks in the voice of an Enlightenment philosopher, having educated himself through reading, among other things, Milton and Goethe. His is an eloquent plea for parental love and recognition, and to be afforded the Rights of Man. The Monster demands our sympathy, and most readers of the novel find themselves ready to give it, only to realize that the Monster is effectively using his highly advanced rhetorical skills to justify the unjustifiable, the trail of corpses (specifically, the dead women and children) he has left in his wake. So toxic, in fact, is the Monster's speech that the novel needs to contextualize it

Figure 8. Abraham Bosse's frontispiece to Thomas Hobbes, *Leviathan* (1651).

within several layers of framing narrative, like the shielding around a radioactive core. At the centre of the novel, he tells his story to Victor Frankenstein, who in turn tells his story to the polar explorer Robert Walton, who in turn tells his story to his sister Margaret Saville.

Frankenstein's politics are similarly double-edged. The novel, we have seen, is a product of the fervour of revolutionary Europe. The novel's central metaphor of the Monster, an eight-foot giant made up of the parts of many men, is an image with a distinct political pedigree. Abraham Bosse's famous frontispiece to Thomas Hobbes's *Leviathan* (1651)

(Figure 8)—the philosophical treatise which insists on the necessity of strong centralized authority in order to curb and regulate the riotous, anarchic, self-destructive capacities of humanity—shows an image of the monarch as a giant made up of many tiny people, the body of the state, illustrative of Hobbes's assertion that 'A multitude of men, are made one person, when they are by one man, or one person, represented; so that it be done with the consent of every one of that multitude in particular.'

Edmund Burke, the great anti-revolutionary theorist, consistently throughout his writings used the image of the monster as a metaphor for the dangerous forces let loose by revolution. In October 1789 he wrote to his son of 'the portentous state of France—where the Elements which compose human society seem all to be dissolved, and a world of Monsters to be produced in the place of it'. France and its revolutionary government is described variously in his writings as 'a monster', a 'monster of a state', the 'mother of monsters', a 'monstrous compound', and a 'cannibal republic'; Jacobinism is nothing but a 'monstrous fiction'. In his *Letters on the Proposals for Peace with the Regicide Directory of France* (1796–7), Burke wrote: 'out of the tomb of the murdered monarchy in France has arisen a vast, tremendous unformed spectre, in a far more terrifick guise than any which yet overpowered the imagination, and subdued the fortitude of man'. This in turn seems to have informed the celebrated, and highly Gothic, opening sentence of Marx and Engels's *Communist Manifesto* (1848): 'A spectre is haunting Europe—the spectre of communism. All the powers of old Europe have entered into a holy alliance to exorcise this spectre.' Victor Frankenstein has let loose a monster on the world, but the novel will not commit to an interpretation of this action.

Subsequent iterations of the *Frankenstein* story tended to smooth out these ambiguities and ambivalences. The central problem of the Monster's persuasive speech was elided by rendering him effectively mute. Boris Karloff's almost wordless performances in James Whale's *Frankenstein* (1931) and *The Bride of Frankenstein* (1935) are iconic and as powerful as anything in cinema, but his Monster is no Enlightenment philosopher.

Film versions have also tended to be very clear as to what they understand as the nature of mad scientific transgression. In a spoken preface to Whale's *Frankenstein* (1931), Edward Van Sloan explains, 'We are about to unfold the story of Frankenstein, a man of science who sought to create a man after his own image, without reckoning on God.' As the creature comes to life, Colin Clive's Henry (*sic*) Frankenstein exclaims, 'It's alive! It's alive! Oh, in the name of God! Now I know how it feels to be God!' (This last line was considered so inflammatory that it was replaced by a thunderclap, and only restored in later reissues.) In *The Bride of Frankenstein*, Dr Pretorius (Ernest Thesiger) offers Frankenstein a toast 'To a new world of gods and monsters!' Cinematic mad scientists are forever playing God. Charles Laughton's Dr Moreau in *The Island of Lost Souls* (1932) claims he knows 'what it feels like to be God'—an entirely plausible spin on H. G. Wells's original novel, which the author himself described as a 'theological grotesque'. In *The Raven* (1935), Béla Lugosi's neurosurgeon Dr Vollin describes himself as 'a god tainted with human emotions'. In the 1958 original of *The Fly*, Al Hedison's scientist is warned that his research is 'frightening. It's like playing God.' And so on. From *Frankenstein* onwards, mad scientists are hubristic monsters. Like Prometheus, they are demiurges, stealing the power of the gods to create life.

Technophobia

As the nineteenth century turned into the twentieth, horror's scientific narratives began to incorporate specific anxieties about the rise of scientific specialization. This was a development which took the concerns and the language of scientists very far from those of non-scientists, and led to fears of the unchecked, antisocial powers of what Sagan called 'morally feeble technologists', pursuing disinterested scientific research for its own sake, heedless of the consequences. In an age of superweapons, nuclear power, genetic engineering, man-made climate change, and mass surveillance, scientific advances have given us much to be afraid of, not least because we live with their consequences without understanding them.

When the Royal Society was founded in 1660 as the major British learned society for the advancement of scientific knowledge, part of its initial remit was the formalization of a specialized scientific *language* in which to report its discoveries, and although these linguistic strictures took a long time to be accepted absolutely, by the close of the nineteenth century they certainly were. In 1791, the natural philosopher Erasmus Darwin published *The Botanic Garden*, perhaps the last major scientific treatise to be written in verse. When, in 1859, his grandson Charles published *The Origin of Species*, which was, as we have seen, probably the single most revolutionary book of the nineteenth century, he made sure that it was written in a style that was accessible to the educated lay reader. *The Origin of Species* was in its turn heavily influenced by the formulation of geological deep time in Charles Lyell's *Principles of Geology* (1833), a work which was something of a bestseller. But works such as these stand out against the tenor of their times, which saw scientific theory become increasingly distant from the concerns, and even the comprehension, of most Victorians. Few, if any, non-scientists could hope to understand the intricacies of the great late-century physicist James Clerk Maxwell, for example, let alone the work of Albert Einstein, who has settled in the public imagination as the archetypal remote, abstract scientific genius.

This opened up a fissure, what was to become known as the 'two cultures' model, after the controversial series of Rede Lectures given by C. P. Snow in 1959. As both a chemist and a novelist, Snow had a foot in both camps, and thus felt himself able to comment with sympathy and authority on the division he saw opening up:

> I believe the intellectual life of the whole of western society is increasingly being split into two polar groups . . . . Literary intellectuals at one pole—at the other scientists, and as the most representative, the physical scientists. Between the two a gulf of mutual incomprehension—sometimes (particularly among the young) hostility and dislike, but most of all lack of

> understanding. They have a curious distorted image of each
> other. Their attitudes are so different that, even on the level
> of emotion, they can't find much common ground.

The notion of a scientific and a humanistic culture viewing one another with mutual incomprehension and suspicion was ripe for exploitation in horror. This sense of cultural distance and dislocation has contributed to a characteristically modern horror discourse, the technophobic narrative, in which 'the machines' rise up and enslave or destroy humanity. Technophobic narratives of this kind generally exist on the cusp of two major and increasingly closely interrelated genres, horror and science fiction.

Killer robots of various kinds have long been a staple of science fiction. Gort, the intergalactic humanoid superweapon controlled by Michael Rennie's Klaatu in *The Day the Earth Stood Still* (1951), is one of many popular cultural responses to the political and existential crisis caused by the atomic bomb in the post-war decades, from the city-destroying Godzilla to the giant ants of *Them!* (1954) or the protagonist of *The Incredible Shrinking Man* (1957), increasingly tiny and powerless as a result of his exposure to a mysterious mist. Gort itself is an unstoppable destroyer that can only be deterred by the abort code, 'Klaatu barada nikto'. In Stanley Kubrick's *2001: A Space Odyssey* (1968), the sentient computer HAL 9000 attempts to take over the ship and destroy the crew. (Perhaps not ironically, HAL is by far the most human thing about Kubrick's brilliant but notably cold and stylized film.) In Donald Cammell's *Demon Seed* (1977), Julie Christie is impregnated by sentient supercomputer Proteus IV, in what is effectively a techno-phobic adaptation of *Rosemary's Baby*. In *The Terminator* (1984) and its various sequels, Arnold Schwarzenegger's indestructible cyborg is sent back in time, originally to destroy and then later to protect key figures in the human resistance to Skynet, a self-aware supercomputer system which has superseded human civilization. In *The Matrix* (1999), contemporary reality is the fictional creation of a computer programme, while machines battery-farm humanity for a source of energy.

Terminator 2, released in 1991 after the end of the 1980s, a decade notable for its nuclear nightmares, makes the Bomb central to its dystopian vision. Skynet is given control of defence systems in order to preclude the possibility of 'human error', and unleashes a nuclear Armageddon. 'Now I am become death, the destroyer of worlds.' These, reportedly, were the words that the chief scientist of the Manhattan Project, J. Robert Oppenheimer, said to himself after testing the first atomic bomb in the New Mexico Desert on 16 July 1945. (Oppenheimer, realizing the implications of what his Los Alamos team had achieved better than anybody, was later to disavow atomic weapons, and became a powerful opponent of nuclear proliferation.) Cultured man that he was, Oppenheimer was quoting from the *Bhagavad Gita*, and perhaps summoning up a memory while doing so of the work of T. S. Eliot, who had studied Sanskrit at Harvard, and for whom the *Bhagavad Gita* was a major source of inspiration—and what person of culture in the mid-twentieth century, musing on the Bomb, would not have thought of *The Waste Land*?

But Oppenheimer's musings were too abstruse to speak to the public imagination. And so it was that, a couple of decades later, at the height of the Cold War, in March 1966, edition number 48 of Stan Lee and Jack Kirby's Marvel superhero comic book *The Fantastic Four* saw the coming of Galactus, the planet-devouring interstellar deity, whose arrival on earth was foreshadowed by his herald, the Silver Surfer. Now *this* was 'death, the destroyer of worlds' given a form the general public could really understand—gigantic, all-powerful, not so much hostile to humanity as completely indifferent to human affairs (Figure 9). Galactus was terror incarnate. And he was not, in fact, Marvel's first engagement with the Bomb.

Figure 9. Galactus: 'death, the devourer of worlds'.

The Fantastic Four's own powers stem from their exposure to 'cosmic rays' as they attempt to beat the Russians in the space race ('Ben, we've got to take that chance, unless we want the commies to beat us to it'). In 1962, young Peter Parker was bitten by an irradiated spider, and developed superhuman powers: the Amazing Spider-Man had arrived. Appearing a year later in 1963, the X-Men are human mutants, yet another reaction to the possibility of irradiated mutation. (In this version of popular culture, at least, exposure to radiation will give you superpowers rather than cancer.) Most strikingly of all, in May 1962, nuclear scientist Dr Bruce Banner was accidentally caught in the blast-zone of a nuclear test (the Bomb was set off by a communist saboteur). Rather than being vaporized, as you might think, Dr Banner's body absorbs the 'gamma radiation' (the most powerful form of electromagnetic radiation: Lee and Kirby are not altogether making this up), which transforms him into an unstoppable raging colossus, the Incredible Hulk. What is the Hulk, if not the Bomb made flesh? A major figure of modern popular culture, the superhero, though superficially far removed from horror, derives in part from an oblique engagement with the implications of nuclear weapons.

But whatever their origins, we are expected to celebrate the superheroes, in a way that is far too blithe and unconsidered for the edgy appeal of horror. In its incorporation of flesh and machine, the cyborg is a better representative contemporary figure. The cyborg is another of horror's liminal boundary transgressors: flesh/machine; human/inhuman; living/inorganic; sentient/algorithmic; familiar/strange. In 'The Uncanny', Freud gives a sustained reading of

E. T. A. Hoffmann's 'The Sand-Man', for him the definitive uncanny tale, whose narrator falls in love with an automaton, which he believes to be a living girl. A 'doll which appears to be alive', Freud writes, is a major source of the uncanny; 'a particularly favourable condition for awakening uncanny feelings is created when there is uncertainty whether an object is alive or not, and when an inanimate object becomes too much like an animate one'. Given this, it is not surprising that one significant effect of computer-generated imagery is known as 'uncanny valley', describing the sense of displacement or even revulsion that audiences feel in the presence of human simulacra that, in their very lifelikeness, are utterly, frighteningly inhuman.

In the Introduction, I discussed the way in which *Unfriended* explores the impossibility for the millennial generation of a meaningful life offline. In the same way, it seems that our contemporary Victor Frankenstein is not a mad scientist as such, but a computer geek. Brilliant, callow, nihilistic, and plutocratic, this figure is emblematic, or even symptomatic, in modern popular culture, from Robert Downey Jr's Tony Stark to Jesse Eisenberg in *The Social Network* (2010) to Oscar Isaac in *Ex Machina* (2015). In this last film, Isaac plays the CEO of Blue Book, an all-conquering search engine, who creates Ava (Alicia Vikander), a beautiful android who is, like Frankenstein's Monster, in equal measures utterly sympathetic and ruthlessly murderous. Ava is the authentic creation of a post-millennial Modern Prometheus.

6

Afterword

Horror Since the Millennium

Where is horror today? Throughout this book, I have tried to stress the cultural proliferation of horror, and its plurality. Horror is tentacular, spreading everywhere. It is Protean, taking many forms. It manifests multiple personalities and has been put to many uses, made to suggest or articulate a variety of positions, ideologies, arguments, and worldviews, not all of them consistent and some of them downright contradictory. While some, including myself, would argue that horror is at its most powerful when it is at its most confrontational—violating taboos, flowing over boundaries, antagonizing respectability—there is no doubt that some of the finest horror shores up traditional worldviews.

But some of the finest horror also comes from the margins. It arises out of the peripheral, the regional, the provincial, the neglected, the discarded: from *Wuthering Heights* to *The Texas Chain Saw Massacre*, occluded identities insist on their presence. Some is deliberately cheap and shoddy, an affront to aesthetic as well as moral and social norms; it is the product of single-minded, bloody-minded independent film-makers, or reclusive, autodidactic writers who seem to be trying to remake the world, but are really addressing only themselves, and perhaps a tiny handful of cultish devotees.

The classic example of this is H. P. Lovecraft, writing in solitude in Rhode Island and barely noticed by any cultural establishment during his own lifetime. M. R. James, the most establishmentarian of horror writers, was scornful of Lovecraft, maintaining that his 'style is of the most offensive'. It is easy to see why. Lovecraft is, by any traditional literary standards, the author of some of the worst prose ever committed to print. 'Squamous', 'gibbous', 'eldritch', 'obscene', 'hilarious', 'tenebrous', 'Cyclopean': you never get far in his writings before coming across a characteristically purple Lovecraftian adjective. When I started teaching Lovecraft to undergraduate students in the 1990s, one of the unexpected pleasures of doing this was getting the class to compare our various editions of the stories, in creased and dog-eared, velvety paperbacks from forgotten publishers, each with a more lurid cover-image than the last. Whatever Lovecraft was, he was not respectable. Today, Lovecraft's works are widely available in editions published by major academic and commercial publishers, impeccably edited, annotated, and introduced, sometimes by distinguished university professors. In 2005, the Library of America, the great national canon-making institution, published its edition of his works. H. P. Lovecraft has *arrived*.

Like all processes of incorporation, the canonization of Lovecraft is double-edged. Recognition means respectability, and respectability is the very thing much horror exists to confront. But academic respectability is largely a harmless affair. More troubling is the incorporation of horror within consumer culture. This is not, of course, a qualitatively new phenomenon—like all forms of popular culture, horror has often eagerly sought its own marketization. But the accelerated incorporation of marginal identities since the millennium threatens the depoliticization of horror, and has led to the creation of a type of horror which has no possibility of ever being horrifying. I want to call this *unhorror*.

Unhorror resembles horror, and deploys, often in a very self-conscious and accomplished way, many of horror's tropes. Its vampires are better looking and have sharper fangs. Its metamorphoses are seamless, using computer-generated imagery to transform its monsters in a way which comprehensively outdoes the attempts of the previous generation of make-up and visual effects artists. Its monsters are bigger and more destructive, from the city-wasting *kaiju* of *Cloverfield* (2008), *Pacific Rim* (2013), or *Godzilla* (2014) to the most recent iteration of King Kong, *Kong: Skull Island* (2017), whose giant ape is at least twice the size of the 1933 original—and, we are told, still growing.

With the success of *Twilight*, I have suggested, horror became totally incorporated within capitalism. As a vehicle for marketing, including the mass marketing of itself, much post-*Twilight* unhorror falls firmly within the purview of what Adorno called the culture industry: like pre-digested baby food (to return to Adorno's metaphor), it is art which does the thinking for its audience, and ideally allows no space for even the possibility of opposition. As such, it is not disturbing or scary, except perhaps to a Marxist.

Indeed, the critic Catherine Spooner has identified a contemporary mode which she terms 'Happy Gothic', suggesting that 'Contemporary Gothic can increasingly be termed as comic, romantic, celebratory, gleeful, whimsical, or even joyous.' Spooner is quite correct here, and her analysis of this phenomenon is smart, illuminating, and nuanced, closing with an assertion of her belief that there remains a space within contemporary Gothic for 'a counter-narrative... in which the tastes of women, children, teenagers, queer and subcultural communities are of particular significance'.

It is certainly the case that horror appeals to more than one audience, and that the tastes of these audiences may not be compatible. The young adult audiences for paranormal romances such as *Twilight*, or for Charlie Higson's zombie books, or Darren Shan's *Cirque Du Freak* and *Demonata* books, or Patrick Ness's brilliant dystopian novels, are not the same audiences as each other, let alone the same audiences as those who once thrilled to *The Texas Chain Saw Massacre* or *The Evil Dead*. Perhaps, also, it's the case that any identity can ultimately be commodified. But what's missing is any sense that this contemporary Gothic is *horrifying*. Can it be that a 'comic, romantic, celebratory, gleeful, whimsical... joyous' cultural mode has replaced one which is obnoxious, rebarbative, confrontational, grotty, transgressive, nasty, and dangerous? If so, we have lost much, if only temporarily.

It is customary, in overviews such as this, to survey the current scene of one's subject and pronounce upon its multifarious complexity, as though this was some radical departure from a smoothly univocal tradition in the past.

I have tried to show throughout the book that horror has *always* been complex, multifaceted, contradictory, and (at its best) troubling. Nevertheless, any attempt to capture the contemporary state of horror can only remark upon how disparate it seems.

A viewer of mainstream Hollywood horror cinema in the early twenty-first century might well have concluded that the genre, in this manifestation at least, was creatively moribund. Cinematically, the US film industry appeared content to allow younger directors to plunder its back catalogue of horror films in what seems like an endless (re)cycle of sequels, remakes, and reboots, a corporate production line of unhorror, a waste land. Most particularly, American cinematic horror revisited landmark films of the 1970s, the key decade for American horror (in a 2016 *Time Out* 'experts' poll' of 'The 100 Best Horror Films', six of the top ten were from the 1970s, and a further three from 1968, 1980, and 1982). There were, for example, remakes of *The Texas Chain Saw Massacre* (2003), *The Hills Have Eyes* (2006), and *Carrie* (2013), and even, unbelievably, of two of the most notorious films in the ultra-controversial rape-revenge subgenre, *The Last House on the Left* (2009) and *I Spit on Your Grave* (2010). Some of these 1970s films, in and around their original release, were viewed as genuinely dangerous cultural artefacts, drawing the horrified gaze of legislators, judges, censors, cultural commentators, and the media. Their post-millennial counterparts tend to come and go unnoticed, because they don't matter.

Whatever one may think of them, these 1970s originals were marked by a kind of demonic energy, made by

143

film-makers operating far from the mainstream, with a great singleness of purpose and vision. These films were at least honestly sleazy. They even had, in their appalling way, a kind of integrity. While some of these films may have been reprehensible, they were not quite indefensible. In fact, in her enormously influential study of horror cinema, *Men, Women and Chain Saws*, the critic Carol J. Clover offered an intellectually coherent reading of perhaps the worst of them, Meir Zarchi's infamous 1978 film *I Spit on Your Grave*, as being at the very least no worse than many mainstream films containing sexual violence, which tend to excite little commentary or controversy. Potentially, the film was even available for a reclaiming feminist analysis. *I Spit on Your Grave* certainly does not glamourize rape: its shocking scenes might be read as an attempt at a representation appropriate to the magnitude of the crime; the film's point of view throughout is that of the woman, Jennifer Hills (Camille Keaton). It is a painful, violent, horrific film about pain, violation, and horror.

In part this recycling is understandable, as the cultural consumers of one generation age into the cultural producers of the next, and revisit the works with which they grew up. The director and musician Rob Zombie, for example, is clearly besotted by and intellectually indebted to American 1970s independent horror cinema, whose tropes and images he reproduces in films such as *House of 1000 Corpses* (2003), *The Devil's Rejects* (2005), *Lords of Salem* (2012), and *31* (2016), which are best viewed as 1970s pastiches (complete with cult period actors such as Karen Black, Sid Haig, Michael Berryman, Judy Geeson, and Ken Foree). Viewers of Zombie's empty *Halloween* (2007) might conclude that the creativity and imagination of John Carpenter's landmark 1978 slasher had been replaced by a mean-spirited nihilism.

Oran Peli's *Paranormal Activity* (2007) was the most successful American horror film of the twenty-first century up until the release of *It* in September 2017. In profit-to-budget terms, it is perhaps the most successful film of all time. Viewed in isolation, the film is an exemplar of post-millennial unhorror. It relies on a 'found footage' technique which, following the success of *The Blair Witch Project* (1999), had been overused in horror cinema to the point of cliché. (And *Blair Witch* itself, although undeniably brilliant, had adapted its own found footage technique from *Cannibal Holocaust*.) It began a self-recycling franchise, which has produced six films to date. There is nothing distinctively contemporary about this, nor is it inherently problematic. I have already argued that this element of repetition is an important component of the ritual aspect of horror, and the notion of a cinematic horror franchise goes back as far as Universal Studios in the 1930s. But viewed in the context of a horror cinema which seemed to have run out of ideas, this repetition may be just another sign of creative bankruptcy.

Paranormal Activity is also the foremost exponent of the cinematic technique which is most characteristic of post-millennial unhorror, the jump-shock—long periods of tense silence punctuated by loud noises (what the film critic Mark Kermode has termed the 'quiet-quiet-BANG!' technique, and sometimes known in cinematic parlance as 'the Bus', in honour of a celebrated scene in the 1941 Val Lewton–Jacques Tourneur film *Cat People*, in which a scene of great tension is broken by the loud hiss of a bus's brakes).

This is undeniably effective, but as a dominant aesthetic technique it is neither terror nor horror in the way that these terms have come to be understood. Anyone can sneak up behind you, shout 'BOO!' very loudly, and make you drop your ice cream. But this says nothing about the state of your soul, your place in the universe, the social function of violence, the evils of political inequality, or any of the other serious questions horror is accustomed to asking.

Not all contemporary horror is unhorror; and even unhorror can be resisted. This can be done by reading its products wilfully against the grain of their intentions, or by reading them not as individual works but within larger cultural and political trends and patterns, or by seeking out those works which are (still) produced far from the mainstream. A sense of critical purchase is even possible on *Paranormal Activity*. As the Introduction argued, horror often works contextually, giving oblique forms to cultural anxieties. Released in 2007, the year of the global financial crisis, *Paranormal Activity* may now be best viewed as the precursor of a modern economic horror, in a series of films focusing on the themes of property, inheritance, home invasion, or a more generalized financial anxiety. Though very different films, *Drag Me to Hell* (2009), *You're Next* (2011), *Dream House* (2011), *Would You Rather* (2012), *The Tall Man* (2012), *The Purge* (2013), and *mother!* (2017) all revolve around these fundamentally economic anxieties. Christine, the protagonist of Sam Raimi's *Drag Me to Hell*, is cursed by an elderly woman whose house is to be repossessed after Christine refuses her application for a mortgage extension. The protagonists of *Paranormal Activity*, Katie and Micah, move into their new house in San Diego, and begin to be terrorized by a supernatural entity. Significantly, Micah is in financial services, working from home as a day trader. A reading of these films in the context of post-millennial economic horror might understand their supernatural visitations as a form of retributive justice.

Nor is this phenomenon confined to film. In Paul Tremblay's startlingly metafictional novel *A Head Full of Ghosts* (2016), the family of Marjorie, an adolescent girl whose behaviour suggests she may be possessed by a demon, agree to take part in a reality TV show. Totally immersed within horror culture, the novel succeeds in being more than the sum of its many intertexts—*The Amityville Horror*, Stephen King, Shirley Jackson, Mark Z. Danielewski's *House of Leaves*, Lovecraft, *The Exorcist*, and much else besides, including *Paranormal Activity* itself—because of its solid grounding in the lived reality of post-crash economic life. Marjorie's father, Josh Barrett, has recently been made unemployed:

> The family's financial situation, like so many other folks, was in the shitter, shall we say. Barrett had worked for the toy manufacturer Barter Brothers for nineteen years but was laid off after Hasbro bought out the company and closed down an eighty-year-old factory in Salem . . . . There was only so much stretching the Barretts could do to maintain two daughters and a big house and a real estate tax bill and all the hope and promise that comes with the middle-class lifestyle.

Set against the background of 'DC politicians, angry Occupy Wall Street protestors, Tea-Party rallies, unemployment charts and graphs', the Barretts' is a 'new and all-too-familiar American economic tragedy'. In order to support their precarious middle-class status, the family invites the TV cameras in.

If one strain of contemporary American political horror is economic, then understandably another is ecological. President Donald Trump's decision in 2017 to withdraw America from the Paris Agreement on climate change action followed a sustained campaign of climate change denial by the American right, which brought together the economic interests of certain parts of corporate America with the cultural anti-modernity of the Evangelical religious right. Unusually, horror's response to this denial has been virtually univocal: climate change is real; the earth is warming; this is a man-made disaster; our survival is under severe threat. Thus, for example, in M. Night Shyamalan's *The Happening* (2008), plants begin to release toxins which are deadly to humanity. Construction worker Curtis (Michael Shannon) begins to have apocalyptic visions of a coming storm which will devastate humanity in Jeff Nichols's *Take Shelter* (2011). The film closes with drops of black rain (oil?) falling from the sky. Steroid-laden excrement dumped into Chesapeake Bay from an industrial chicken-rearing plant creates a mutated strain of flesh-eating parasites in Barry Levinson's genuinely disturbing *The Bay* (2012). The film is an extrapolation of real-life environmental concerns that manure run-off from intensive poultry farms was contributing to a number of ecological 'dead zones' in Chesapeake Bay. In Jeff VanderMeer's novel *Annihilation* (2014), a team of scientists investigates the mysterious Area X, a sealed-off area of unknowable nature. VanderMeer's novel has been compared to the work of the great American philosophical ruralist Henry David Thoreau, whose 1851 book *Walden* is the great American literary meditation on the relationship between humanity and the natural world.

Given widespread anxieties about the melting of the polar ice caps, it is not surprising that the twenty-first century has produced a good deal of Arctic and Antarctic horror. Polar Gothic is a recurring subgenre of horror. Drawing on the long-unexplored and thus fundamentally *imaginary* geography of the polar regions, a number of works of horror (and also of fantasy) have been set in the far northern or southern latitudes. The narration of *Frankenstein* takes place on board the ship of the polar explorer Robert Walton. At the close of the novel, Victor Frankenstein heads out on the ice, towards the North Pole, in pursuit of his Monster. Edgar Allan Poe's only novel, *The Narrative of Arthur Gordon Pym of Nantucket*, follows its protagonist on his inexorable journey south, towards its Antarctic climax. Fresh out of medical school, Arthur Conan Doyle served for a time as a doctor on a Greenland whaling ship; his story 'The Captain of the Pole-Star' is an imaginative response to this voyage. Heavily influenced by Poe, Lovecraft's great novella *At the Mountains of Madness* charts the terrifying discoveries of an Antarctic expedition. All three film versions of *The Thing* (1951, 1982, 2011), based on John W. Campbell's 1938 novella, *Who Goes There?*, are set in polar latitudes (Antarctica in 1938, 1982, and 2011, Northern Alaska in 1951).

Polar horror, then, is not a new phenomenon, but it has gained exponentially in intensity in the last decades. Roland Emmerich's *The Day After Tomorrow* (2004) opens in the Antarctic, where a slice of the ice shelf 'the size of

Rhode Island' breaks off due to global warming, a harbinger of the climatic disaster to follow, in which the northern USA becomes uninhabitable, and Mexico gives shelter to American refugees. This was the film which spurred former Vice President Al Gore to make his own influential climate change documentary film, *An Inconvenient Truth* (2006). In 2017, a slice of the Antarctic Larsen C ice shelf did break off: it was larger than Delaware, which itself is half as large again as Rhode Island. In Larry Fessenden's film *The Last Winter* (2006), an ecohorror reimagining of Algernon Blackwood's classic work of Canadian horror 'The Wendigo', the melting of the permafrost releases supernatural entities, first into a remote oil-drilling camp on the Northern Slope of Alaska, and then, it is implied, worldwide. When Abby (Connie Sellers), the camp's only survivor, wakes up in hospital, she hears news reports about a widespread disaster; a doctor in the room next door has hanged himself. Stepping outside, she walks through puddles of water: the snow has melted.

The hospital in which Abby wakes is presumably in Barrow, Alaska, the northernmost city in the US. Barrow's isolation, cut off from the world for long periods, is what makes it vulnerable to a vampire attack in *30 Days of Night* (2007). *The Last Winter*'s trope of the melting polar ice releasing forces inimical to humanity recurs in *The Thaw* (2009)—with Val Kilmer as a climate scientist—and the TV series *Fortitude* (2015–17). *Fortitude* was set in the Svalbard archipelago, the northernmost inhabited place in the world. Svalbard is also the setting for parts of Philip Pullman's young adult fantasy *Northern Lights* (1995), and for Michelle Paver's remarkable retro ghost story, *Dark Matter* (2010). In

Game of Thrones (broadcast from 2011), the Night King and his zombie army sweep down from the frozen north, laying waste to the ice wall that has kept them at bay for millennia, and threatening to wipe out humanity.

America's racial divisions have also begun to find expression in post-millennial horror. The African American writer Victor LaValle's novella *The Ballad of Black Tom* (2016) is a rewriting of H. P. Lovecraft's 'The Horror at Red Hook', one of the most racist stories by a writer whose racism was notoriously toxic. Recasting Lovecraft's tale as the story of a Harlem musician, Tommy Tester, who gets drawn into an occult world, LaValle's work records his own ambivalence towards Lovecraft—the dedication reads 'For H. P. Lovecraft, with all my conflicted feelings.' Robert Suydam, the protagonist of 'The Horror at Red Hook', confronts Tester in characteristically racist Lovecraftian terms: 'Your people are forced to live in mazes of hybrid squalor. It's all sound and filth and spiritual putrescence . . . . Policemen despair of order and see rather to erect barriers protecting the outside world from the contagion'. Tester dismisses this: 'You talking about Harlem? . . . I'm trying to understand what in the hell place you're talking about. It doesn't sound like anywhere I've ever lived.'

Initially, the premise of Jordan Peele's *Get Out* (2017) resembles that of Stanley Kramer's *Guess Who's Coming to Dinner* (1967), in which Katharine Hepburn and Spencer Tracy play a wealthy, liberal San Francisco couple, the Draytons, forced to confront their own prejudices when their daughter brings home an African American fiancé (Sidney Poitier). The first half of *Get Out* plays like an awkward comedy of manners, in which Daniel Kaluuya's Chris endures the embarrassing but apparently well-meaning attentions of his girlfriend's wealthy, liberal parents, the Armitages (Bradley Whitford and Catherine Keener). As well as *Guess Who's Coming to Dinner*, *Get Out* has also been compared to the socially aware 1960s and 1970s horror of Ira Levin, most particularly *The Stepford Wives* (1972), which stands alongside Stephen King's *Carrie* (1974) as an uneasy, ambivalent male response to the women's liberation movement. In *Get Out*, the seemingly tolerant wealthy whites are still exploiting black America—both the Draytons in 1967 and the Armitages in 2017 have African American domestic workers. Whitford's Dean Armitage is a neurosurgeon who has literally devised a means of turning black people into white people. The film uses this plot device simultaneously to examine American racial and class divisions, the unconscious racism of liberal, white America, and the consequences of African American suburbanization and *embourgeoisement*.

The fifty-year symbolism of 1967 and 2017 is also exploited in Kathryn Bigelow's *Detroit* (2017). Though not ostensibly a horror film, *Detroit* borrows heavily from the home invasion/torture porn subgenre in its account of the imprisonment, torture, and murder of innocent African Americans at the hands of racist white cops during the 1967 Detroit riots (the film's recounting of the events of 25 July 1967 is based on fact, as are most of its characters). Bigelow certainly has a provenance as a director of horror: she made her reputation with the vampire film *Near Dark* (1987), and then cast *Halloween*'s 'scream queen' Jamie Lee Curtis in the lead role in the psycho thriller *Blue Steel* (1989).

Bigelow is also skilled at combining genres in her films: *Detroit* is a political drama and a horror film, as *Near Dark* is a vampire film and a road movie, and *Blue Steel* a psycho film and a police procedural (and *Point Break* is a kind of existential surfing crime thriller). The violence, brutality, and injustice of *Detroit*'s middle act, set in the Algiers Hotel, are truly horrifying, almost unbearable. *Detroit* is a film which speaks very clearly to the current state of America. The film's point is that law and justice in America is institutionally racist, and no contemporary viewer can watch this film without thinking of the killing of Michael Brown in Ferguson, Missouri, or of Trayvon Martin, Antonio Martin, Tamir Rice, Eric Garner, or numerous other young black men in the 2010s at the hands of the police. *Detroit* is as much a film about Trump's America as it is about Lyndon B. Johnson's.

Outside the US, post-millennial British horror has been examining its own national identities, part of a historical-political trend that began with the Northern Irish peace process and the Scottish and Welsh devolution referenda in the 1990s, and progressed through to the Brexit referendum of 2016. Folk horror, a subgenre rooted in the land, its folklore, superstitions, and pagan past, often inflected with a heavy dose of Frazer's *The Golden Bough*, is the major post-millennial manifestation of this, as well as partaking in some of the ecohorror concerns we have been discussing.

Folk horror is fundamentally antagonistic to urban technological modernity, and has its contemporary origins in the ruralist and localist countercultural movements of the 1960s. The original iteration of folk horror in the 1960s and 1970s, though certainly not recognized as any kind of coherent artistic movement at the time, included, for example, the novels of Alan Garner, whose often very disturbing young adult ruralist works included the neo-Arthurian *The Weirdstone of Brisingamen* (1960), the extraordinarily folkloric *The Moon of Gomrath* (1963), and two works with their origins in Welsh mythology, *Elidor* (1965) and *The Owl Service* (1967). It would also include, emphatically, films such as *Witchfinder General* (1968), *The Blood on Satan's Claw* (1971), and *The Wicker Man* (1973), as well as a number of television plays and series, from Granada TV's very weird adaptation of *The Owl Service* (1969), to *Robin Redbreast* (1970), *The Exorcism* (1972), *Penda's Fen* (1974), and the terrifying *Children of the Stones* (1977), and the various adaptations of M. R. James broadcast under the *A Ghost Story for Christmas* banner across the 1970s. All of this seemed to be a response to post-war modernization, and as such did not survive into the neoliberal era ushered in by the election of Margaret Thatcher in 1979.

Post-millennium, British popular culture has revisited the possibilities of folk horror, often with a strong awareness of what Robert Macfarlane has called, in an essay of the same title, 'The eeriness of the English countryside'. Sometimes very strikingly, the films of Ben Wheatley have incorporated folk horror. *Kill List* (2011) begins as a political thriller about a pair of hitmen, and ends as a *Wicker Man*-style exercise in pagan horror. *Sightseers* (2012) reimagines Mike Leigh's *Nuts in May* (1976) as a tale of a pair of caravanning serial killers. The indescribable *A Field in England* (2013) self-consciously revisits the English seventeenth century of *Witchfinder General*, *The Blood on Satan's Claw*, and James's

'The Ash Tree' (broadcast as a *Ghost Story for Christmas* in 1975). In Elliott Gardner's frightening *The Borderlands* (2014), a pair of Catholic priests investigate apparent paranormal events in a remote Devon church, only to discover that the land itself contains (or is) a powerful pre-Christian entity. Beginning with the Welsh nationalist horror novel *Candlenight* (1991), Phil Rickman has written a highly knowledgeable series of folk horror novels, many of them set on the English-Welsh border and featuring the Anglican exorcist Merrily Watkins. On television, the relationship between the cosy and the menacing was explored in *The League of Gentlemen* (1999–2002), whose fictional northern village of Royston Vasey was the setting for stories that were funny and frightening in precisely equal measure. *A Ghost Story for Christmas* returned in 2005, with adaptations of the James stories 'A View From a Hill' (2005), 'Number 13' (2006), 'Whistle and I'll Come to You' (2010), and 'The Tractate Middoth' (2013).

The revived interest in M. R. James is part of a more general British resurrection of old-school horror. Michelle Paver's arctic ghost story *Dark Matter* (2010) is a reminder of how genuinely frightening the uncanny can be. Neil Spring's *The Ghost Hunters* (2013) retells the story of Harry Price's investigation into Borley Rectory, 'England's Most Haunted House'. Andrew Michael Hurley's *The Loney* (2015) is as haunted by its Lancashire landscape as James's work was by East Anglia.

Much of the most inventive and influential horror of the last generation, certainly in the cinema, has been non-Anglophone. Asian horror has become particularly important, beginning with a series of startlingly original and effective Japanese horrors, leading to the classification of the so-called J-horror (Japanese) and K-horror (Korean) subgenres.

Hideo Nakata's *Ring* (1998) may be the single most influential horror film of contemporary times. The film established an influential modern paradigm of a malevolent, unappeasable female ghost (white nightdress, long black hair covering her face) (Figure 10) in a film which combined the traditional ghost story and the curse narrative (a familiar trope in horror, from *The King in Yellow* to 'The Monkey's Paw' to *Night of the Demon* to *Candyman*) with an ingenious use of (then-)modern technology, the VHS tape which spells death to all who watch. *Ring* was adapted from a novel by

Figure 10. Sadako, the unappeasable ghost of *Ring* (1998).

Koji Suzuki, whose work also provided the source material for Nakata's *Dark Water* (2002), another female ghost story, set in a leaking apartment building. *Audition* (1999), Takashi Miike's psycho horror, contains an acupuncture scene so horrifying that when I saw it in the cinema, the entire row in front of me all got up and left at the same time. Takashi Shimuzu's *Ju-on: The Grudge* (2002) is another tale of a vengeful female ghost, again using the familiar iconography of Japanese horror (the hair, the white shift, the disjointed movement). The commercial and critical success of these films created a market in the West for Asian horror cinema more generally, as well as for the inevitable Hollywood remakes. *Ring*, *Dark Water*, and *The Grudge* were all adapted for an American audience, as was the lauded Korean ghost story, *A Tale of Two Sisters*, remade in 2009 as *The Uninvited*. Contemporary Hollywood's attempt to incorporate these Asian visions into itself in this series of remakes was invariably underpowered and disappointing.

Rather different from the main tendency of contemporary Asian horror, Kinji Fukasaku's *Battle Royale* (2000) is a work of dystopian horror. An economic crash precipitates a regime of severe population control, one aspect of which is that a class of high-school students are transported to an island and made to fight to the death. This is a recurring trope in horror, dating at least from Leslie Banks's man-hunting exiled Russian aristocrat Count Zaroff in *The Most Dangerous Game* (1932); *Battle Royale*'s premise also clearly anticipates the *Hunger Games* series of books and films. The film is in equal measures voyeuristic, fascistic, and critical of that voyeurism and fascism, and, with its subject matter of murderous adolescents, was itself the subject of a minor moral panic. It was banned in several countries, and, while never formally banned in the US, was not officially released there until 2012.

There have also been important works of Hispanic horror. The Mexican director Guillermo del Toro made his reputation in the 90s with the stylish and original vampire film *Cronos* (1993), before moving to Hollywood to direct the entomological horror *Mimic* (1997). But it was with two Spanish-language films set against the backdrop of the Spanish Civil War and its Francoist aftermath that del Toro really made his reputation: the ghost story *The Devil's Backbone* (2001) and the uncategorizable *Pan's Labyrinth* (2006), which was placed at or near the top of many critics' lists of best films of its year. *Pan's Labyrinth* very self-consciously recalls classics of weird fiction, most particularly Arthur Machen's *The Great God Pan* and Algernon Blackwood's *Pan's Garden*, as well as one of the landmark works of Spanish cinema, Victor Erice's *The Spirit of the Beehive* (1973), whose child protagonist, Ana, uses James Whale's *Frankenstein* (1931) as a means of understanding the political reality of early Francoism, just as *Pan's Labyrinth*'s child protagonist, Ofelia, uses the film's fantastic underworld as a means of understanding the same context.

Produced by del Toro, the Spanish director J. A. Bayona's haunted house film *The Orphanage* (2007) is a masterly example of a traditional ghost story adapted to modern cinema. The sensibilities of *[REC]* (2007) are altogether more contemporary. Like so much post-millennial horror, *[REC]* is a found footage film. Set entirely in a Barcelona apartment building which has been sealed off by the authorities owing to an outbreak of a rabies-like zombification virus, Jaume Balagueró and Paco Plaza's electrifying film draws much of its effect from its extraordinarily traditionalist fidelity to the classical dramatic unities of place, time, and action—one building, one night, one relentless narrative.

Where, finally, is horror today? The location of horror moves with culture, I have argued. We may be seeing signs that it is moving, with geopolitics, away from an American axis. It may also be that, in our concentration on horror's traditional media, fiction and film, we have been, if not looking in the wrong places, then certainly not looking in *all* the right places.

When it was released in 1992, Fran Rubel Kuzui's film *Buffy the Vampire Slayer* received mixed reviews, and passed without much notice. Unsatisfied with both the film and its reception, its writer Joss Whedon tried again, adapting it for television. The first episode of *Buffy the Vampire Slayer* was broadcast on 10 March 1997, with Sarah Michelle Gellar, an authentic nineties 'scream queen', in the title role (in that same year, 1997, she appeared in the neo-slashers *I Know What You Did Last Summer* and *Scream 2*). Looking back from the perspective of twenty years, it is tempting to view this moment as marking a tectonic shift in American horror. Playing over seven seasons (1997–2003), *Buffy* developed into a work, and a world, of considerable complexity, intelligence, and imagination, the very antithesis of the risk-averse, compromised, moribund condition of much mainstream cinematic American unhorror around the millennium, which seemed incapable of ever surprising or delighting its audience.

Buffy also came into being with the internet, and so its success was greatly augmented by the rise of the blogosphere, and by the online culture of fandom. It also captured the academic imagination: the sub-discipline of 'Buffy studies', combining institutional academic criticism and theory with fandom and unlicensed criticism in the public sphere, has produced a small library of often very sophisticated cultural and textual analysis.

Buffy was one of the early signs that the millennial generation was experiencing what is often characterized as a (or *the*) Golden Age of television, from *The Sopranos* (1999–2007) to *The Wire* (2002–8) to *Breaking Bad* (2008–13) to *Game of Thrones* (2011–18). The medium has shed much of its cultural inferiority complex relative to film. First broadcast in 2013, *Hannibal* took the continuing story of our great modern demon to creative heights seemingly foreclosed to film versions after Brett Ratner's unforgivably lumpen 2002 adaptation of *Red Dragon*. With seasons entitled 'Murder House', 'Asylum', 'Coven', 'Freakshow', 'Hotel', 'Roanoke', and 'Cult', *American Horror Story* (first broadcast in 2011) engages with the satisfyingly familiar tropes and locations of horror. The Louisiana-set first season of *True Detective* (2014) drew explicitly on the history of American weird fiction, most particularly with its references to the lost land of Carcosa, originally to be found in Robert W. Chambers's *The King in Yellow* and in the works of Ambrose Bierce.

However, from a historical perspective this Golden Age of television might come to be viewed as a last gasp. Certainly, it is a product of the moment in which the dominant cultural medium of the second half of the twentieth century,

160

television, began to be subsumed within the dominant cultural medium of the twenty-first, the internet.

What might authentic internet horror look like? One place to look might be at podcasts such as the hugely enjoyable fake radio show *Welcome to Night Vale* or the riotously inventive *Down Below the Reservoir*. The brilliance of these podcasts rests on the rather twentieth-century notion that they are produced and controlled by highly creative auteurs (Joseph Kink and Jeffrey Cranor for *Night Vale*, Graham Tugwell for *Reservoir*). Another distinctive internet product, meme culture, has the potential to be altogether more decentred and anarchic. It may be uncontrollable.

Here is one example. On 10 June 2009, a pair of photoshopped images appeared on *Something Awful*, a comedy website and online forum. Credited to Victor Surge, the photographs showed two groups of children, photographed in black and white. In the background, blurred and indistinct, was a tall figure dressed in black, and seemingly with tentacles for arms. This was the Slender Man (Figure 11). Beneath the images were these captions:

> 'we didn't want to go, we didn't want to kill them, but its persistent silence and outstretched arms comforted us and surrounded us at the same time...'
>
> 1983, photographer unknown, presumed dead

> One of two recovered photographs from the Stirling City Library blaze. Notable for being taken the day which fourteen children vanished and for what is referred to as 'The Slender Man'. Deformities cited as film defects by originals. Fire at

library occurred one week later. Actual photograph confiscated as evidence.

> 1986, photographer: Mary Thomas, missing
> since June 13th, 1986.

Lacking any kind of central controlling narrative beyond a vague but palpable sense of menace and threat, particularly to children, the Slender Man took on a life of its own as a self-replicating, evolving internet meme, recurring first in user-generated 'creepypasta' online fiction and art, and in YouTube videos, video games, and more generally as an elusive cultural referent. On 31 May 2014, two twelve-year-old Wisconsin girls stabbed a classmate nineteen times after a night reading online Slender Man creepypasta. They did this, they said, in order to become the Slender Man's servants, or in the language of the internet, his 'proxies'. Fears that the Slender Man seems capable of infecting

Figure 11. The Slender Man.

reality, and transforming it, have led to the most recent of horror's ongoing series of moral panics. The case went to trial in September 2017. The defence attorney claimed the girls had 'swirled down into madness together'. The defendants, Morgan Geyser and Anissa Weier, were sentenced to forty years and twenty-five years in mental hospitals, the maximum sentences possible for their respective crimes.

The internet is too vast, and too fast, for a book of this size. It has given horror an infinite library in which to play, an endless labyrinth in which to hide. The Slender Man is its most distinctive monster thus far. He is the scariest thing in ages. But there will be others.

FURTHER READING

Quotations from classical texts throughout are from the Loeb Classical Library editions. Quotations from the Bible are from the King James Version.

All references to Freud are to *The Standard Edition of the Complete Psychological Works of Sigmund Freud*, 24 vols, ed. and trans. James Strachey et al. (London: Hogarth Press/ Institute of Psychoanalysis, 1955).

INTRODUCTION

Some of the arguments in the early part of this chapter are informed by Rene Girard, *Violence and the Sacred*, trans. Patrick Gregory (London: Continuum, 2005). The insights of Mary Douglas, *Purity and Danger* (London: Routledge, 1966) inform the whole of this book. For palaeohistorians and the importance of art for the formation of *Homo sapiens*, see, for example, Ronald Hutton, *Pagan Britain* (New Haven and London: Yale University Press, 2013), chapter 1; Jill Cook, *Ice Age Art: Arrival of the Modern Mind* (London: British Museum, 2013); Yuval Noah Harari, *Sapiens: A Brief History of*

Humankind (London: Vintage, 2011), part 1. For ritual, see Clifford Geertz, 'Religion as a Cultural System', in *The Interpretation of Culture: Selected Essays* (London: Fontana, 1993). For moral panics and video nasties, see Stanley Cohen, *Folk Devils and Moral Panics* (London: MacGibbon and Kee, 1972); David Kerekes and David Slater, *See No Evil: Banned Films and Video Controversy* (Manchester: Headpress, 2000); Martin Barker and Julian Petley, eds, *Ill Effects: The Media/Violence Debate*, 2nd edition (London: Routledge, 2001). For the Gothic, see Fred Botting, *Gothic* (London: Routledge, 1996); Nick Groom, *The Gothic: A Very Short Introduction* (Oxford: Oxford University Press, 2012). Stephen King's writings on horror can be found in *Danse Macabre: The Anatomy of Horror* (London: Futura, 1982) and *On Writing: A Memoir of the Craft* (London: Hodder and Stoughton, 2000). For the uncanny, see Sigmund Freud, 'The "Uncanny"' (*Works*, vol. 17). For the weird, see Mark Fisher, *The Weird and the Eerie* (London: Repeater, 2016). For the 'culture industry' and popular culture, see Theodor Adorno, *The Culture Industry*, ed. J. M. Bernstein (London: Routledge, 1991); Curtis White, *The Middle Mind: Why Consumer Culture is Turning Us Into the Living Dead* (London: Penguin, 2003); John Storey, *An Introductory Guide to Cultural Theory and Popular Culture* (Hemel Hempstead: Harvester, 1993); Dominic Sandbrook, *The Great British Dream Factory: The Strange History of Our National Imagination* (London: Penguin, 2015). The major work on sociophobics is David L. Scruton, ed., *Sociophobics: The Anthropology of Fear* (Boulder: Westview Press, 1986). For the classic account of reverse colonization, see Stephen Arata, *Fictions of Loss in the Victorian Fin de Siècle: Identity and Empire* (Cambridge: Cambridge University Press, 1996). See also Patrick Brantlinger, *Rule of Darkness: British Literature and Imperialism, 1830–1914* (Ithaca: Cornell University Press, 1988).

CHAPTER 1: MONSTERS

For general studies of monsters, see Jeffrey Jerome Cohen, ed., *Monster Theory: Reading Culture* (Minneapolis and London: University of Minnesota Press, 1996); Stephen T. Asma, *On Monsters: An Unnatural History of Our Worst Fears* (Oxford: Oxford University Press, 2009); Marina Levina and Diem-My T. Bui, eds, *Monster Culture in the 21st Century: A Reader* (London: Bloomsbury, 2013). Freud's writing on taboo can be found in *Totem and Taboo* (*Works*, vol. 13). For an excellent overview of cannibalism, see Jennifer Brown, *Cannibalism in Literature and Film* (London: Palgrave Macmillan, 2013). For a hugely influential reading, see William Arens, *The Man-Eating Myth: Anthropology and Anthropophagy* (Oxford: Oxford University Press, 1979). The best single work on vampires remains Nina Auerbach's *Our Vampires, Ourselves* (Chicago and London: University of Chicago Press, 1995). Christopher Frayling, *Vampyres: Lord Byron to Count Dracula* (London: Faber, 1992) is an invaluable guide and sourcebook. For the folkloric vampire, see Paul Barber, *Vampires, Burial and Death: Folklore and Reality* (New Haven: Yale University Press, 1988). For an account of the vampire's journey to the cinema, which includes the quotation from Maxim Gorky, see David J. Skal, *Hollywood Gothic: The*

Tangled Web of Dracula from Stage to Screen (London: Deutsch, 1990). Much less has been written on zombies, but Roger Luckhurst, *Zombies: A Cultural History* (London: Reaktion, 2015) is superb.

CHAPTER 2: THE OCCULT AND THE SUPERNATURAL

For Weber on disenchantment, see Max Weber, 'Science as a Vocation', in *Max Weber: Essays in Sociology*, trans. and ed. H. H. Gerth and C. Wright Mills (Oxford and New York: Oxford University Press, 1958). Conan Doyle's comments on spiritualism are from Arthur Conan Doyle, *The New Revelation and the Vital Message* (London: Psychic Press, 1981). For general studies, see Janet Oppenheim, *The Other World: Spiritualism and Psychical Research in England, 1850–1914* (Cambridge: Cambridge University Press, 1985); Christopher Partridge, *The Re-Enchantment of the West: Alternative Spiritualities, Sacralization, Popular Culture, and Occulture*, 2 vols (London and New York: T&T Clark, 2005–6). For magic, see Éliphas Lévi, *The History of Magic Including a Clear and Precise Exposition of its Procedure, its Rites and its Mysteries*, trans. Arthur Edward Waite (London: William Rider, 1922 [1860]); Lynn Thorndike, *A History of Magic and Experimental Science During the First Thirteen Centuries of Our Era*, vol. 1 (New York: Columbia University Press, 1923). For the section on the Devil, I draw heavily on Jeffrey Burton Russell, *The Devil: Perceptions of Evil from Antiquity to Primitive Christianity* (Ithaca: Cornell University Press, 1977). See also

Peter Stanford, *The Devil: A Biography* (London: Heinemann, 1996); Gareth J. Medway, *Lure of the Sinister: The Unnatural History of Satanism* (New York and London: New York University Press, 2001); Darren Oldridge, *The Devil: A Very Short Introduction* (Oxford: Oxford University Press, 2012); Ruben van Luijk, *Children of Lucifer: The Origins of Modern Religious Satanism* (Oxford: Oxford University Press, 2016). Everyone should read Rollo Ahmed, *The Black Art* (London: Senate, 1994). Much has been written on ghosts and the ghost story, but for this chapter I have particularly drawn on Owen Davies, *The Haunted: A Social History of Ghosts* (London: Palgrave, 2007). For a comprehensive modern critical account, see Scott Brewster and Luke Thurston, eds, *The Routledge Handbook to the Ghost Story* (London: Routledge, 2017).

CHAPTER 3: HORROR AND THE BODY

Sabine Baring-Gould, *The Book of Were-Wolves* (London: Smith, Elder & Co., 1865) is a fascinating book. Freud's 'Wolf Man' is discussed in 'An Infantile Neurosis' (*Works*, vol. 17). For fairy tales, see Bruno Bettelheim, *The Uses of Enchantment: The Meaning and Importance of Fairy Tales* (London and Harmondsworth: Penguin, 1978); Marina Warner, *From the Beast to the Blonde: On Fairy Tales and their Tellers* (London: Vintage, 1995). David Cronenberg's interviews can be found in Chris Rodley, ed., *Cronenberg on Cronenberg* (London: Faber and Faber, 1997); Clive Barker's are collected at <http://www.clivebarker.info/interviewsindex.html>. For a philosophical study of the emptiness of torture, see Bob Brecher, *Torture and the Ticking Bomb* (Oxford: Blackwell, 2007); for a psychological study demonstrating its inefficacy for information-gathering, see Shane O'Mara, *Why Torture Doesn't Work: The Neuroscience of Interrogation* (Cambridge, MA: Harvard University Press, 2015).

CHAPTER 4: HORROR AND THE MIND

For madness as a social problem, see Michel Foucault, *Madness and Civilization* (London: Routledge, 2001); R. D. Laing, *The Divided Self* (Harmondsworth: Penguin, 1970). For Victorian asylums, see Sarah Wise, *Inconvenient People: Lunacy, Liberty, and the Mad-Doctors in Victorian England* (London: Vintage, 2013). Psychoanalytic accounts of the double can be found in Freud, 'The "Uncanny"', and in 'On Narcissism: An Introduction' (*Works*, vol. 14), and in Otto Rank, *The Double: A Psychoanalytic Study*, trans. Harry J. Tucker (Chapel Hill: University of North Carolina Press, 2012 [1914]). Horror and the suburbs is discussed in Bernice Murphy, *The Suburban Gothic in American Popular Culture* (Basingstoke: Palgrave, 2009). For influential analyses of the slasher movie, on which I draw here, see Vera Dika, 'The Stalker Film 1979–81', in Gregory A. Waller, ed., *American Horrors: Essays on the Modern American Horror Film* (Urbana and Chicago: University of Illinois Press, 1987); Carol J. Clover, *Men, Women and Chain-Saws* (Princeton: Princeton University Press, 1992).

CHAPTER 5: SCIENCE AND HORROR

The quotations from Carl Sagan are all from *The Demon-Haunted World: Science as a Candle in the Dark* (London: Headline, 1997). For the 'two cultures', see C. P. Snow, *The Two Cultures and the Scientific Revolution* (Cambridge: Cambridge University Press, 1959). For scientific materialism (or naturalism), see Gowan Dawson and Bernard Lightman, eds, *Victorian Scientific Naturalism: Community, Identity, Continuity* (Chicago and London: Chicago University Press, 2014). Popular cultural mad science is discussed in Roslynn D. Haynes, *From Faust to Strangelove: Representations of the Scientist in Western Literature* (Baltimore: Johns Hopkins University Press, 1994); David J. Skal, *Screams of Reason: Mad Science and Modern Culture* (New York: W. W. Norton, 1998); Christopher Frayling, *Mad, Bad and Dangerous? The Scientist and the Cinema* (London: Reaktion, 2005). The information on Faust is from Leo Ruickbie, *Faustus: The Life and Times of a Renaissance Magician* (Stroud: History Press, 2009). The section on the politics of monstrosity in *Frankenstein* and beyond draws heavily on Chris Baldick, *In Frankenstein's Shadow: Myth, Monstrosity, and Nineteenth-Century Writing* (Oxford: Clarendon Press, 1987).

AFTERWORD: HORROR SINCE THE MILLENNIUM

For contemporary Gothic, see Catherine Spooner, *Post-Millennial Gothic: Comedy, Romance and the Rise of Happy*

Gothic (London: Bloomsbury, 2017). For ecohorror, see Bernice M. Murphy, *The Rural Gothic in American Popular Culture: Backwoods Horror and Terror in the Wilderness* (London: Palgrave Macmillan, 2013); Andrew Smith and William Hughes, eds, *Ecogothic* (Manchester: Manchester University Press, 2013). For an impressive overview of folk horror, see Adam Scovell, *Folk Horror: Hours Dreadful and Things Strange* (Leighton Buzzard: Auteur, 2017); see also Robert Macfarlane, 'The Eeriness of the English Countryside', *The Guardian*, 10 April 2015. For TV horror, see Helen Wheatley, *Gothic Television* (Manchester: Manchester University Press, 2006); Lorna Jowett and Stacey Abbott, *TV Horror: Investigating the Dark Side of the Small Screen* (London: I.B.Tauris, 2013).

INDEX

Index

From bloody Greek tragedies to violent films and spooky stories, we have been enjoying the thrill of horror for thousands of years.